Southern Sage
The Honorable Woodrow Melvin
By
Sylvia Melvin

Cindy,

Thank you,

Sylvia Melvin

This is a true story. None of the names have been changed and all of the events happened as related to the author by Woodrow Melvin, his family, friends and work associates.

Contact:

Sylvia's Scripts

Sylvia Melvin
6053 Arnies Way
Milton, FL 32570
(850) 626-8778

Email: sylviamelvin@earthlink.net
www.sylviamelvin.com
Blog: http://sylviasscribbles.blogspot.com

ISBN: 1452850879
EAN-13: 978-1452850870

Webster's Collegiate Dictionary defines the word sage as a mature or venerable man of sound judgment.

This book is dedicated to Judge Woodrow M. Melvin, a man who personified these characteristics. His devotion to public service and respect for the laws of our nation were exemplified in a career that included attorney, Representative in the Florida State House of Representatives and State Senate, Circuit Court Judge and Appellate Court Judge.

Acknowledgments

Many thanks to the following people who generously gave of their time in order that I could tape the memories, stories, opinions and feelings so openly expressed. You provided the raw material; I simply arranged the words:

Rev. Joe Bamberg
Beulah Chabal
Gloria Prescott Clubb
Ray Helms
T.Sol Johnson
Kathy Jordan
Lillian Kelley
Jeanelle Kingry
Butch Lindsay
Judge George Lowery
Dr. Hiram(Mac) Melvin
Jim Melvin
Laura Melvin
Woodrow Jr.(Mac) Melvin
Nita Melvin
JudgeWoodrow M. Melvin

Since this edition of "Southern Sage" is a rewrite, some of the men and women I interviewed have deceased but their contribution to the story lives on.

Thank you, one and all.

Sylvia Melvin

Preface by Laura Melvin

The Honorable Woodrow M. Melvin

When I was asked to write the preface to this book, the problem was obvious. How do you write a preface to an old sage? Particularly when that very southern sage was your father, your friend, your mentor?

I was blessed to know Woodrow M. Melvin, first through the eyes of an adoring child growing up in his home and later as I served as an attorney and then judge, modeling much of my professional and personal life after his. I know something of his strengths and weaknesses: his willingness to reach, to deal with the world expansively rather than from the safety of preconceived ideas; his private stumbles which to the few who were genuinely close served as rude reminders that he was after all, still a man.

Dad would routinely wake up at night with ideas tossing around in his head about a particularly difficult case he had heard. He reached many decisions in the wee hours of the night with Orders scratched out on whatever paper was close to the night stand. After he had the case figured out and the Order written, Dad would go into a very relaxed sleep, and get up the next morning whistling. He became renown for his legal writings-concise with interesting phrases. His writings are easy to read and show few traces of the time and anguish he devoted to each decision.

The Honorable Woodrow M. Melvin was also a gentle man with a warm and sensitive heart. This was always an asset in his role as father of five, but not always in his job as trial judge. As a judge, part of his routine was to mete out justice and punishment, but he did so with respect to all. Regardless of the press of his schedule, he was always willing to listen. Judge Melvin saw children as special gifts and invested much of himself in the effort to insure that their best interest was served.

With rare courage, Dad opened his heart to his family, work, and world. Surely his heart and soul were scarred by what he saw and experienced over the years, and yet, he grew even wiser. The passage of time generated a relentless and resolute multitude of physical problems which he met head on, looking each one squarely in the eye, choosing time and again to do everything possible to live. His spirit never gave up, in fact never died, but finally, to quote the sage himself, "In response to the inexorable laws of nature", the body of this warm and compassionate judge passed on, leaving much behind—including his happy whistle, in the train coming down the track, in the wind playing in the top of the pine trees, in the waves folding onto the beach.

Introduction by Sylvia Melvin

For more than twenty years, the name Woodrow Melvin meant little to me. Since we lived many miles apart, I'd never met him, spoke to him or even seen a photo of him. All I knew about this man was that he lived in Florida, he was a judge and my husband was his nephew. In August of 1993, after our family moved to Florida, I met Woodrow on a sultry, Sunday morning in a little country church. Sitting in the pew beside me was a senior gentleman that looked like a man in a family photo I'd recently found. After the service, I leaned over and asked, "Excuse me, are you Judge Melvin?"

From the moment his face broke into that warm, welcoming smile, I felt I'd met a friend. The invitation to 'come on down' and visit him and Aunt Nita, his wife, was sincere and I accepted with anticipation. Within minutes we began catching up on each other's lives and any formality dissipated with laughter and conversation. After the hugs and good-byes, the door was not closed behind me but instead, Uncle Woodrow and Aunt Nita stood on the porch and watched me get safely into my car. As I swung around in the driveway, I looked back once more and they waved a last adieu. In the ensuing months, the ritual did not change; I came to realize a visitor was always welcomed at their door and never rushed away. It made a warm impression upon my heart.

As I got to know Uncle Woodrow, and learned more about his life in public service, I realized here was a man who made a difference in the lives of the people of Florida. But not everyone was privileged as I was to sit and hear the stories of the early years of practicing law, the many sessions he spent helping to shape state laws or the multitude of criminal and civil court cases he heard as a Circuit Court Judge. Due to Uncle Woodrow's failing health, history was slipping through the fingers of Santa Rosa County. Someone needed to compile a record of this man's accomplishments. As a free-lance writer, I welcomed the task.

Peeling away the layers of time through the research was a

journey that not only educated and enlightened me but revealed insight into the personality of a man, who because of his modest nature, never boasted of his servitude. Family scrapbooks, newspaper articles, micro-film, interviews with secretaries, court clerks, lawyers, judges, family and friends presented a wealth of information. The most valuable source was Woodrow himself. As he responded to the questions I asked, memories of years gone by came to light and I was able to record his personal reaction to whatever the particular circumstance. At times, his body language verbalized as plainly as the spoken word.

In order to give a well-rounded picture of Woodrow's life, I felt it necessary to bring the reader along historically, too. Therefore, references are made to the many newspaper articles written about important issues he was involved in.

I have only one regret; our time together was too short—Woodrow died sixteen months after our first meeting. There was so much more about the man I wanted to know.

Thank you Uncle Woodrow, for showing me not only the meaning of genuine southern hospitality, but also a true Southern Gentleman.

Part One

Chapter One
Perseverance

"There it is; there it is!" Nita Melvin's shaking finger pointed to the name, Woodrow Maxwell Melvin, printed in the Sunday Florida Times Union newspaper under the headline: Florida Bar Announces Graduates.

"Woodrow, you're a full-fledged lawyer." Nita's arms circled her husband's neck and she hugged him. "I knew you could do it. All your hard work and determination has paid off."

"Wait just a minute, now darlin'. We were told we'd receive a telegram before any names appeared in the newspaper. No telegram's been delivered to this address. Could have been a misprint, you know."

Nita pulled back and looked into her husband's worried eyes. All summer, the suspense of whether he'd passed the bar exam weighed as heavily on Woodrow's shoulders as the thick, August air.

"I don't believe that for a second; somethin' has happened to it. You know how things get lost or sent to the wrong place. Now stop stewin' and let's enjoy ourselves this afternoon. We'll get to the bottom of this tomorrow."

Nita's optimistic prediction came true when Woodrow picked up his mail Monday morning. Enclosed in an envelope was a telegram dated August, 25, 1935. It had been delivered to his father's address in Milton and David forwarded it to his son in Madison.

Eager to hang his 'shingle' and start practicing law, Woodrow gave a month's notice as Cherry Lake Sawmill's bookkeeper and, with the money he'd saved and his wife at his side, he journeyed back to Milton. Evidence of depressed economic times along the route met them at every railroad stop. The smell of smoke from the hobos' bonfires seeped through the cars and, as the train chugged forward, shadows of gaunt men lunged toward the open freight cars hoping to ride the rails. Vagrants milled around the station begging for money as the words to a popular song, 'Buddy, Can You Spare A Dime?' played on a radio behind the ticket counter.

The clickety-click of the train wheels lulled Woodrow into a reverie and his mind returned to 1930 and his first yearning to become a lawyer. As a teenager, he assisted his father, a county tax assessor, by typing the tax rolls at the court house. As he passed the doors of the courtroom each day, his curiosity was piqued. He began slipping into a bench at the back of the room to watch the trials. As he listened to the lawyers present their arguments and observed the evidence presented to the jury, a desire to become one of them ignited inside him and he made a decision. "I can do that."

Although his mind was made up and he was eager to pursue his dream, reality threatened to thwart his plans. In a family of six sibling brothers, with the eldest in medical school, there was no money to extend his education beyond a secretarial and court reporting course given at Pensacola Business School.

Upon graduation nine months later, with diploma in hand, a dauntless Woodrow applied for and was hired as a legal secretary for a Milton lawyer, Franklin West, at a salary of three dollars a week. Knowing Woodrow's quest to become a lawyer, Mr. Franklin gave him ample opportunity to ask questions and pour over the law books lining the shelves of the office.

The small salary underscored Woodrow's need for additional funds to enable him to reach his educational ambition. Lucky for him, 1931 brought a new opportunity to add to his coffers and strengthen his hope of attending law school when he accepted a position working in the secretarial pool for the sixty-day legislative session in Tallahassee. This time his salary was six dollars per day which he faithfully put into the First National Bank in Milton to pay for a three-year correspondence course in law from LaSalle Extension University of Chicago.

The day President Roosevelt ordered all the banks in the country to close down to take an inventory, Woodrow wondered how he could overcome this new roadblock and pay the seven-dollars monthly tuition. Fate intervened when the university took mercy and notified students that they would accept whatever money they could send.

Santa Rosa County's decision to expand highway 87 north couldn't have come at a more opportune time as far as Woodrow was concerned. Hired as a time keeper at eighty dollars a month, he knew law school was within his grasp. In 1934, he enrolled as a new student from Milton, Florida, at Cumberland University School of Law in Lebanon, Tennessee, renowned for its number of alumni who sat as judges on the benches of federal and state courts.

The constant motion of the train chugging along the track had a hypnotic affect on his mind and memories of his days studying for his law degree flooded his conscientiousness. He could never forget Dean Caruthers with his white, flowing beard and thundering voice. Simply the thought of this man caused Woodrow to instinctively sit upright in the cushioned train seat and straighten his tie. Dean Caruther's words at the first student welcoming assembly were imprinted in Woodrow's mind.

"You are sitting here in two groups," intoned the Dean. "There are those of you who have come up here to learn and you're going to get along pretty good and the other group of you are those who have come from wealthy families and you've come up here to play and maybe think it's a thrill to go to law school. I'll be sending you back home in a few weeks."

Woodrow shook his head in wonderment as he recalled the faces of those that fell into the latter group. Hard work and

3

sacrifice brought him to that campus and he had no intentions of forfeiting his dream.

A smile worked across Woodrow's cherub-like face as he remembered his naïve understanding of Tennessee winters, and a shiver ran through his five-foot-seven-inch slender frame. Walking a mile and a half from his boarding house in four or five inches of snow, wearing a pair of low quarter shoes, resulted in wet socks and cold feet. A big, pot-bellied stove stood in the middle of a large classroom and one of the professors, who realized that the boys from the south were not used to Mother Nature's winter whims, allowed them to wring out their socks, dry them close to the heat, and prop their feet up while he went on with his lecture.

The months of lectures, tests and work on term papers flew by and before Woodrow knew it graduation was penciled in on his 1935, May calendar. At the commencement ceremony, attended by friends, family and one-hundred and thirty-eight graduates, Woodrow accepted recognition that he graduated with an average of ninety-four percent. His heart swelled with pride for the school that was now his Alma Mater and a tear gathered at the corner of his eye as he read a poem in the program written by a fellow graduate, Foyd Poe.

"Oh, Cumberland, My Cumberland!
Proud may she ever stand.
All hail her past, her history!
All hail her future destiny!
Her walls, her halls are ever dear,
Her noble men we'll e're revere;
Her heart, to our hearts ever near,
Cumberland, My Cumberland!

Graduate of Cumberland School of Law, 1935

With all the pomp and ceremony behind him, Woodrow knew the biggest test lay ahead –the state bar exam. To prepare for it, he and Nita, his bride of six months, moved to Tallahassee to live with her parents while Woodrow attended a cram course given at night by a local attorney. The evening of the final exam, Nita welcomed home an exhausted husband.

"I gave it everything I had, honey. Now we have to wait and see if it was enough."

Nita squeezed his hand in reassurance. "I have no doubt you did. When will you know if you passed?"

"We were told not to look for our results for at least three months. Something tells me it's going to be a long summer. But then, I couldn't start practicing even if I had my license. Got to have money to rent an office; that's the next hurdle. No sense sittin' around these next three months I need a job. Think I'll give Dad a call and see if he's heard of anyone hiring. Might have to dust off the ole shovel—who knows?"

The following day, Woodrow combed through the employment ads in the local newspaper but to no avail. With the country deep in depression, the list was short. However, to

Woodrow's surprise, the next day he received a telegram from a high school friend.

"Listen to this, ladies." He rushed into the kitchen waving the paper in the air, and wearing a smile from ear to ear.

Nita and her mother stopped setting the lunch table and gave him their attention.

"Remember Glenn Wood, Nita? We graduated from high school together."

"Sure. What's he up to these days?"

"Seems he works for a sawmill at Cherry Lake north of Madison. He must have been talking to Dad because he's offered me a job as a book-keeper."

Nita clapped her hands and hopped up and down. "Woodrow! That's wonderful."

"Listen to the salary. Eighty dollars a month! If we're careful, we can save enough to open an office."

"Hurry, run over to the telegraph office and tell him you'll take it. We'll keep lunch warm," Nita insisted.

Woodrow chuckled and put his arm around his wife. "I guarantee you he'll get my answer before the day's over. Let's sit down and say the blessing. I'm feelin' extra thankful today."

A short whistle from the train brought Woodrow back to the present and as they neared their destination, the conductor pulled out his watch and in his rich baritone voice warbled, "Twenty minutes to Milton."

Woodrow felt a stir next to him as Nita snuggled closer to her husband, her eyelids still closed by sleep. He squeezed her shoulder. At age eighteen, he knew in his heart the night he met this slim, attractive, girl with the bouncing brunette curls that someday she'd be his wife.

When they stepped off the train, he took her hand and whispered, "We're home Nita. I've got everything I ever wanted—my law degree and my life's partner. Are you ready? Our journey's about to begin."

Chapter Two
Open for Business

Woodrow straightened his tie several times as he prepared himself for his first day of work at his new office. With his felt fedora hat perched at an angle on his beaming face, he kissed Nita farewell and walked to the First National Bank on Willing Street in Milton. The spring in his step on this October morning in 1935 as he climbed the steps to the second floor meant only one thing—he was eager to slip the key into the door of the office and start to work. The rent was within his budget—seven dollars and fifty cents a month with an additional dollar and a half minimum for electricity.

Not expecting any clients the first day, Woodrow wrapped his jacket around the back of a chair, rolled up his sleeves, dug into the boxes of law books and lined them up in a specific order on the waiting shelves. Stacks of papers he'd collected from Cumberland went into a used cabinet, each sorted and filed in a folder under a special category. His manual typewriter sat on his desk ready for him to strike the first key.

By 11:00 a.m., Woodrow gazed around the room, satisfied with the arrangement of the simple furniture, two wooden chairs, a small table and an oak desk with three drawers on the right-hand side. As he contemplated his next move, to his amazement, a knock came on the door.

"C'mon in," he called.

"Heard you'd set up shop and are ready for business, so I asked around and here I am." A man he'd worked with at Cherry Lake entered.

"What can I do for you Stan?"

"Need a divorce-uncontested. How much would it cost me?"

Woodrow's mind went blank, but he thought fast.

"Listen, I was just on my way to the men's room when you walked in so make yourself comfortable and I'll be right back."

Passing the rest room, Woodrow made a mad dash to the lawyer down the hall and asked, "Can you help me out? I've got a man in my office who wants to know what it costs to get an uncontested divorce."

"Twenty-five dollars and twelve-fifty to cover the court costs." The answer came quickly.

"Thanks, I owe you one."

Woodrow walked back into his office thinking his friend would probably get up and leave after he heard the large amount.

"How would you like to arrange to pay for it, Stan?"

"Just write me a receipt, Woodrow. I've been saving for this day."

When Woodrow shared the news with Nita, they thought they'd hit a gold mine that first day on the job, but reality soon stuck its head around the corner. It was a long time before someone else showed up with any money. Instead, bartering was the order of the day. Each night, Nita greeted Woodrow at the door with her familiar nightly question, "Well, what did we earn today?"

When he gave his frequent answer, "Two gallons of cane syrup for typing up a deed", Nita responded with a sigh, "I believe we have enough syrup for now. I'll see if D.T. Williams grocery store will trade it out for some flour."

One night Woodrow reported to his wife, "I've agreed to defend a client in return for a cow."

"A cow! Now where are we going to tether a cow in the

city?" Nita protested.

"I'll tie it to that pecan tree between us and the neighbors."

A few days later, he shook his head and complained, "Nita, that cow refuses to give milk no matter how hard I pull on her tits. I'm afraid I got the short end of the stick."

Woodrow didn't back out on his word. Instead, he gave the man the best defense he could, but when the jury convicted him, Woodrow grinned to himself, thinking, "Justice prevailed."

***

Woodrow had earned his formal higher education at Cumberland Law School, but he learned about people from his fledgling days of practicing law. As each client brought his own personality into his office—good or bad—Woodrow learned to hone his perception skills.

One night a knock came to the door and a black man stood there anxious to talk to Woodrow.

"Sorry for the late hour, Mr. Melvin, but I's got to talk to you."

"C'mon in and sit down. What's the problem?"

"They's gonna arrest me."

"Why?"

"For stealin' my neighbor's cartwheels. They's sayin' I bin watchin' where he buries his money."

"Well, have you?"

The man shuffled from one foot to another and shook his head back and forth. "Oh, no sir. Not me."

"I charge thirty dollars to defend a case."

"Thank you, sir. I'll be back tomorrow night with the money."

To Woodrow's surprise, his client came back with the fee—thirty cartwheels. As he looked at the silver, part of the stolen property, Woodrow was not about to take any of it. Instead, he talked the man into turning it into the sheriff and telling the judge what happened. Probation didn't exist in those days. Instead, a case was carried over on the docket for a length of time condition on a person's good behavior. In this case, two or three court sessions went by until a judge determined the black man was behaving himself and let him go.

"Nita, if he'd gone to trial, he would have been convicted, sent off, and somebody else would have had to feed his family. When common sense and the law collide, there's trouble."

J.B. Abbott, an old country Justice of the Peace, had planted those seeds of insight into Woodrow's mind. When hearing a case, Abbott set up his courtroom at a hardware store in Jay, Florida where he used a rockin' chair and six empty nail kegs for the jury to sit on and another one for the witness.

Woodrow tried five or six cases at the store before Judge Abbott, one of which involved a man who got in a fight and cut the other fellow he was fighting with—cut him pretty bad. When it came time for the judge to hear it, he ordered the man to get up the money to pay the grocery bill for the injured man's family until the victim got over his injuries. The decision sounded pretty good to the community and that's how it got settled.

Woodrow thought about how the judge had settled the case. On one hand, it seemed to him like the man got off easy, but he realized the real problem was who would feed the victim's family if the culprit was locked up? This way, the guilty party worked and split his income. After turning it over in his mind, how Judge Abbott settled the case sounded like practical horse sense to Woodrow.

Fairness ran deep in his lawyer's code of ethics and it was a troubled Woodrow who walked in the door one evening for supper, plopped his fedora unto a coat hook, undid his tie and proceeded to express his frustration, " Nita, it's not right. Remember I told you I agreed to defend this fellow who's accused of breaking into that little corner store and stealin' $1.32? Well, today they brought my client into court to make his plea dressed in convict clothes with leg chains on so he couldn't run."

"Yes, you said you felt the evidence against him is pretty flimsy. Those black stripes and gray stripes runnin' round and round don't leave much doubt where he's been spending some time, does it?"

"Exactly my point. It's prejudicial; why everyone in that courtroom today are the group his jury will be drawn from. Now tell me, what chance will he have?" Woodrow took his white linen handkerchief and wiped beads of perspiration from his reddening brow.

"So what can you do about it?"

"I already filed a motion for continuance. The judge told me he didn't think they'd recognize him on Wednesday seein' as though this is Monday. Things move pretty fast but we'll see."

He was right; his client got convicted. But after the jury's decision, the light in Woodrow's office burned well past midnight. The clickety-clack of his typewriter keys produced one written appeal to the Supreme Court of Florida after another. Wads of paper filled his waste basket. Appealing to the highest court in the state was something he'd never done and it had to be perfect. His argument needed to be clear, concise and accurate. Finally, satisfied he'd made a convincing appeal, Woodrow slipped the pages into an envelope ready to be mailed to Tallahassee. There was nothing more he could do but wait.

A month later, the Supreme Court's opinion arrived in Woodrow's mail. His eyes fixed on the official seal and his hands trembled as he picked up the letter opener and inserted it into the envelope. Relief coupled with humility washed over his body as he read the words that would become a precedent in future cases tried in Florida:

"In reversing the judgment of the circuit court, the supreme court holds that a prisoner may not be given a fair trial if he is brought into court shackled with chains and wearing convict stripes. Every person is presumed to be innocent of the commission of crime, and the presumption continues until his conviction. Appearance of the accused in stripes might prejudice prospective jurors against him."

With letter in hand, a smile on his face, and a bounce in his step, Woodrow headed for the State Attorney's office. The words 'case dismissed' were the sweetest words he'd heard all day.

Chapter Three
An Itch for Politics

"Run for mayor of Milton! You want to get into politics?"

"Why not, Dad?"

David Melvin raised an eyebrow and looked his son straight in the eye. "Because you're only twenty-three years old. Have you forgotten you once worked for your opponent? T. Franklin West is an experienced lawyer. Folks are lookin' for a man with experience. One year practicing law hardly qualifies, son. They'll say you're still wet behind the ears. Won't make you rich either—seven dollars a month".

"I may be young, but I know I can do a good job. Besides, since my practice is smaller than Mr. West's. I'll have more time to devote to helping improve our town's image."

"Campaigning is hard work, Woodrow. Speeches—a well thought out agenda, lots of handshaking."

"That's where I can use you, Dad. Since you're the tax assessor, you know everyone in town and can introduce me as I make my rounds. I have nothing to lose except some time. C'mon; jump on board. Let's see how far this train will go."

A smile crossed David's face as he glanced at his watch, "Get on over to the courthouse; you've got thirty minutes before it closes to register as a candidate."

For the next several weeks, Nita saw him when he left the

house in the morning and then not again until nearly bedtime. Cold suppers were the order of the day as Woodrow attended every function he could in order to be seen and heard. His youthful energy and quick mind caught the voters' attention and on election night, he nosed out T. Franklin West by the slim margin of 263 to 254 and on October 13, 1936, Woodrow was officially sworn in as Milton's mayor.

A hearty congratulations from Woodrow's father came with some valuable advice. "Listen to the people around town, son. Wouldn't hurt to stop by the café for a cup of coffee now and then and mingle with the folks. You'll soon learn what needs to be done."

His father was right.

One such complaint that reached Woodrow's ears concerned the lack of reverence for the Christmas season.

"You'd think it was the Fourth of July the way those fireworks snap and boom over there on Willing and Oak Street all night long. Somethin' needs to be done to stop those annoying disturbances,"

After conferring with City Council, Woodrow asked the Press Gazette to print his first proclamation.

> *"Mayor Melvin asks safe and sane observance of Christmas holidays"*
>
> *Citizens of Milton are requested to refrain from shooting fireworks of any description upon the following named streets, or upon   public or private property adjacent to: Willing, Simpson and Oak Street. All violators will be dealt with according to law.*
>
> *Let us celebrate the Christmas season as a period of worship and adoration, and not as a time for hilarity and dissipation."*
>
> *Woodrow M. Melvin*
> *Mayor, Town of Milton*

***

The hot, humid, air that stifled the atmosphere during the summer of 1937 only intensified the blanket of hopelessness felt by the nation. The Great Depression sucked the lifeblood out of the economy leaving the State of Florida's coffers empty. Even road maintenance done by the convicts came to an abrupt halt due to depletion of state funds. As Woodrow thought about this situation one evening on his walk home from the office, his eyes surveyed the Blackwater River banks. He could scarcely see the water for the overgrown briar bushes, weeds and vines that ran in every direction. A miniature jungle threatened to strangle the drainage ditches and several neglected, empty lots were thick with wild vegetation that served to hide debris and garbage. The scent of a decayed animal accosted his nostrils; not only was downtown Milton becoming an eyesore but environmentally it was a health hazard to its citizens. Something had to be done and Woodrow made a decision.

Two nights later, he brought the issue before the Town Council.

"Gentlemen, I submit that we get permission from the County Board of Commissioners to bring in the convicts and put them to work cleaning up our town. They aren't being used this summer on the roads so let's give them something to do."

The vote was unanimous: contact the County; get the ball rolling.

Two weeks later, the Press Gazette printed the positive news that set everyone in town to chattering at the corner café.

It's a Good Job!
Tons of Weeds Removed From Streets

People who have been out of Milton for several weeks and who return about now will hardly recognize the town. In fact, if they looked around very much they might get the idea they were in the wrong place altogether. Why? Simply because the town has come out from behind a rank growth of weeds. Through the thoughtfulness of Mayor Melvin, backed by town

15

*council, county convicts, who were about to enjoy a long
drawn-out vacation because of the stoppage of state gas
tax money, have been employed to give the town a
general hair-cut, shave, massage and good rub-down,
and are doing a good job of it.*

*Drainage ditches, have been cleaned out, the banks
nicely fixed up, and the ditches are now doing what they
were supposed to do in the beginning—drain off surplus
water.*

*Tons of grass, tall weeds, trees and other growing
things have been cut from streets and sidewalks, and it
is now possible to see how much of the town there really
is.*

*Another good job is the street-scraping work which
is going on in connection with the clean-up, and which,
when completed, will make the streets fit to drive over
without breaking car springs and generally shaking
everybody to pieces.*

*Yes, sir, it's a good job, and should be kept going
until the town is cleaned and smoothed from stem to
stern and from port to starboard.*

Pleased about the success in improving Milton's physical
appearance, Woodrow extended his concern of those who served
in the community. When he spoke to the Council. He voiced his
opinion.

*It is my belief that our night watchman's salary is
entirely inadequate. He is receiving from the town the
sum of $25.00, that being paid to him in the form of
script. In order to cash this script, he has to discount it
for 15%. I realize that at the present time funds are
short, and for that reason, I could not expect a raise in
salary for that position. However, if it is at all possible
for you to do so I would respectfully request that the
town pay Mr. Hannah by check instead of by script.*

The Council agreed and, after that, the night watchman received his salary in cash.

A grateful man knocked on Woodrow's office door the following morning to report his nightly activity.

"C'mon in."

A smile crossed the watchman's fatigued face as he held out his hand to shake Woodrow's.

"Thank you, Sir, for taken' up for me at the council meeting last evening. Getting' paid in script is tough in these here times. You did my wife and me a big favor and we won't forget it."

"Just want to treat you fair. We need your services to help keep law and order around here."

"Speakin' of such, something I notice more and more every night is gettin' worse. Somebody's gonna get hurt or even killed."

Woodrow's expression grew serious. "What is it?"

"Too many drunk drivers and one-eyed automobiles. Last night over on Canal Street one of them crossed over the sidewalk and nearly hit one of the school teachers out walkin' her dog. Crashed into a tree and smashed the windshield to smithereens. The driver got a doozy of a goose egg but he'll be seeing you in the Mayor's Court today."

"Your right, Mr. Hannah, I've noticed the neglect drivers have about fixing headlights and of course, driving drunk is out of the question. I'll write up a resolution and present it to the Council immediately."

The public read the Mayor's proclamation in the Press Gazette.

In my concern for the safety of the citizens of Milton, fair warning will be given all offenders against laws providing proper lights for automobiles, and those who fail to heed the warnings will be brought into mayor's court. Cars with only one light are a menace. It is my intention to do everything possible to promote safe driving in Milton and to decrease the number of accidents caused by improper lights.

17

When writing a resolution or proclamation, it wasn't unusual for Woodrow to take up a pen in the evening and write while his mind was still on the topic. Often he would ask Nita for her input or opinion. One such evening they'd finished dinner and she was washing the last plate when she noted her husband busily writing in his notebook.

"Writing another resolution?" she asked.

"Not this time, my dear."

"So you don't need my input?"

"Actually, I do. I'm resigning."

"Resigning! But why? You won your second term hands down and I know you can win again. The folks in this town appreciate the way you've helped them."

"I want to broaden my field to include more folks."

"And how do you intend to do that?"

"I'm going to run for county judge."

"Against A.L. Johnson?"

"Yes, so I need you to proof read my letter because the next meeting is Monday evening."

Unsure of her feelings, Nita reached for the paper and read Woodrow's letter to Mr. Forman.

February 27, 1940

Hon. R.P. Forman, President,
Town Council,
Milton, Florida

Dear Mr. Foreman,
   As I have become engaged in county political affairs, I respectfully tender to you this my resignation as Mayor of the town of Milton effective March 1ˢᵗ, 1940.
   It has been a privilege and pleasure to have served my home town in this honorary capacity and I have enjoyed my relationship with the members of the Council and the other officers of the town.

With kindest regards,
Sincerely yours,
Woodrow M. Melvin

In making his formal announcement to run for county judge, Woodrow said, "I shall make a clean, active campaign for the office, and if honored with election, will administer it in a fair, reasonable and impartial manner. I believe that my experience in law work qualifies me to hold this office."

Not everyone agreed; Woodrow suffered his first political defeat and after some disappointment and soul searching he graciously admitted, "Santa Rosa has a good county judge. A.L. Johnson is doing a fine job and the only thing I had to say in my campaign was that he had the job and I wanted it. Now, people aren't going to turn somebody out who is doing a good job. I didn't have enough sense to know that but I do now and it's a blessing I got defeated because there are other things I need to do."

Chapter Four
The Road to Tallahassee

"Well, ain't that somethin'," Woodrow mused aloud as he held out the newspaper and glanced at his wife. "Tom Watson is running for attorney general."

"Who's he?" Nita asked.

"Back in '31, when I was looking for a job typing in the secretarial pool in the legislature, Tom was on the attaché committee and helped me get the position. I owe him a great deal." Woodrow smiled and his blue eyes brightened as he continued, "I believe it's time I renewed our acquaintance."

Within a week, Woodrow and his father drove down to Tampa to meet with Mr. Watson at his campaign headquarters.

"I'm here to repay an old debt and offer my services to help you get elected. My father knows everyone in Santa Rosa County and we're ready to use some foot-leather to get the word out that Tom Watson is the man for the job."

"Can't tell you how much I appreciate your offer, Woodrow. Florida's a big state and often the Panhandle gets a lot less attention from politicians than it deserves. Consider yourself on board."

True to his word, Woodrow, his father and other supporters engaged in a rigorous effort of talking to folks, handing out information and showing allegiance to their candidate for attorney general. Election night proved that their efforts paid off; in January, 1940, Tom Watson arrived in Tallahassee and he took nine assistants along with him—one of which was Woodrow Melvin.

Tom Watson clearly stated his expectations of his aides at their initial meeting.

"Loyalty to the interests of the state, as distinguished from the special interests of any group, is, and will be, the first and paramount duty of each of us. The attorney general is an identity to be supported and backed up by you. Your recognition of this fact and loyalty to him will be appreciated and desired. If at any time you feel, for any reason, that you cannot give this personal loyalty, it is respectfully declared that it becomes your duty to renounce such relationship and resign your affiliation with this office."

No sooner had Woodrow settled himself into the assigned area he shared with another lawyer when the Attorney General asked him to come to his office. Woodrow's pulse beat increased and his palms turned moist with perspiration. Was there a problem? Relief calmed his nerves as Mr. Watson welcomed him.

"Woodrow, I've selected you and Joe Gillen to handle all of the state's criminal appeals."

"Thank you, sir. I appreciate your confidence in me to handle this responsibility."

A year later, January,1941, Woodrow and Joe prepared a brief that put their ability to the test.

"Can you believe we're off to Washington to petition the highest court in our country, Joe?"

"Never expected it to happen to me, Woodrow."

"Thirty minutes to convince eight gentlemen to uphold this murder conviction. No time for speeches—only the facts, nothing but the facts."

The return trip was one of celebration; the state of Florida won.

"This is one appeal I'll never forget, Joe. What an awesome

feeling to have participated in the United States judicial system in the most revered court in the country. And do you know what else impressed me?"

"Can't think of anything better than that, my friend."

Woodrow smiled as he commented, "How 'bout that four inches of snow blanketing Washington. This southern boy won't forget that."

The staff of Attorney General Tom Watson
Woodrow is sitting third form the left-bottom row.

***

"It's a boy, Mamma!" Woodrow's enthusiastic announcement as he swung open the kitchen door caught his mother, Laura, with her hands in the biscuit dough. She quickly wiped them on her apron and gave her son a hug.

"You're a father now, Woodrow. After six years of waiting, you and Nita have been blessed. Let me get the family bible and add my grandson's name; still going to pass along your namesake?"

"Nita wants it that way. Just add Jr., Mamma."

"It won't take but a moment; born September 18, 1941, Woodrow Maxwell Jr. Your life will never be the same, son."

Three months later, in the early dawn of December 7, Pearl

Harbor altered everyone's lives. Men in military uniform marched off to war in droves. Rationing commodities such as gas, sugar, coffee, became commonplace and unnecessary driving was discouraged.

Along the coasts of Florida, cities took measures to dim the amount of light that projected onto the ocean for fear that a merchant ship would be silhouetted, thus setting up a target for a torpedo. If one were staying in a hotel, the shades had to be drawn at night. These black-out conditions affected the flying public as well. In order to tend to the state's business, there were occasions when it was necessary for Woodrow to fly. Passengers were told to keep the window curtains closed and as the aircraft passed over darkened cities, out of the blackness a shaft of light from below illuminated the plane's exterior searching for proper identification. Woodrow whispered a prayer of thanks each time they passed the test.

***

"How would you like to go back to Milton, Nita?" Woodrow's question took his wife by surprise.

"You mean for a visit?"

"No, I mean leave Tallahassee and return to practicing law. We've been here four years and I miss my own practice. If you're in agreement, I'll speak to Mr. Watson tomorrow."

A smile from his wife gave Woodrow the answer. "When do I start packing?"

On their return to Milton, the local newspaper pressed Woodrow for his reason for resignation and received the following answer.

I enjoyed the work in the attorney general's office very much. In the person of Tom Watson, the people of Florida have an outstanding attorney general, and to have had the opportunity to work with him as an assistant has been a keen pleasure to me. It's real good to be back home again. My work during the past four years has brought me into nearly every county in Florida, but of them all, Santa Rosa is my choice.

This time Woodrow hung his shingle on the second floor of the Milton Gazette building. Besides tending to his own law practice, he was hired by the County Board of Commissioners as the county's prosecuting attorney. For the next two years, Woodrow became more and more involved with the Democratic caucus and the instinct to serve the public on a larger scale rose to the surface once again. With Nita firmly supporting his decision, Woodrow formally announced his bid for member of the House of Representatives in the Milton Gazette, March 21,1946:

Political Announcements for Representative

I appreciate this opportunity to announce to you my candidacy for election to the office of Representative of our county in the Florida Legislature.

For the past eleven years, I have been actively engaged in the practice of law and have been admitted for practice in the United States Supreme Court, and the State Courts of Florida. I have served as assistant to the Attorney General of Florida for four years and during that time had the opportunity of working with your State Officials in Tallahassee. I feel that this training and experience, and my knowledge of the problems facing our county and state, well qualifies me to represent your interests in this law making branch of our State Government.

Should you honor me with election to this office, I shall honestly and faithfully represent the interest of all the county.

I sincerely request the favor of your consideration and vote approval.

Cordially Yours,
Woodrow M. Melvin

The race for a seat in the Florida House of Representatives

was on and Woodrow sought his father's advice.

"Dad, I need your counsel on my campaign strategy; you helped me win the mayor's office but this time the stakes are considerably higher. Any advice?"

David was forthcoming, "It's not going to be easy, Woodrow. Winning the primary is the key; you're opposition is strong. Morrison Kimbrough is a respected Santa Rosa farmer and you know Franklin West is no stranger to the folks in this county. Both good men. Roll your sleeves up and prepare yourself for some long campaign days."

"Dad, remember when I was younger I helped drive U.S. Congressman Millard Caldwell, during his campaign, around the county in a one-seater Ford Coupe. We'd go into towns with one of those fog horns, bark a little bit and get a crowd together. Then I'd go around and pass out his literature. Used to take placards into the stores with his picture on them and get the owner to put them in the windows. Must have worked because he got elected to Congress and served several terms. Ended up governor of Florida. I believe I can duplicate his method."

"Have you thought about your platform? Folks want to know what you stand for and how it's going to affect their lives."

"I've drafted a rough copy; let's hammer this out together."

It took the rest of the afternoon but by supper Woodrow had a grasp of each plank he intended to stand on. Nita offered to role play the undecided voter:

"Tell me how you intend to better our schools, Mr.Melvin."

"I'll enact a special law equally dividing Santa Rosa County's share of the race track money between the Board of Public Instruction and the Board of County Commissioners. I'll also work for any other legislation that benefits the education of our children."

"Old people and dependent children and blind folks don't have much help. What can you do for them?"

"They all need adequate provision and I'll sponsor legislation to accomplish this purpose."

"It's hard being a farmer these days; how you gonna help me?"

"I'll support you by funding the farmers markets for livestock and produce. An adequate appropriation for free hog cholera serum should be made. Gasoline used in farm tractors and other non-highway machinery should be relieved of gasoline tax."

Nita continued, "The county needs more highways and better maintenance."

"I agree and without it our county will not develop its potential."

"Mr. Melvin, if I'm old enough to fight in a war, why can't I vote?"

"You would if I had my way; the voting age should be lowered from 21 to 18. Those who are old enough to fight for their country are old enough to vote."

"You've told me things you're for, now tell me what you're against."

"Useless spending of state money by State Boards, Bureaus and Commissions. A State Purchasing Department, efficiently operated, would save the taxpayers many thousands of dollars on supplies purchased for the operation of the state government. I'm also against a stock law, a sales tax and I'll oppose any legislation harmful to our county or state."

Nita clapped her hands and shouted, "You got my vote," but lowered her voice and continued, "but I guess I'm a little biased." She followed up with a kiss on her husband's cheek.

***

Since a world war had recently been fought to preserve freedom of speech and the right to choose the candidate of one's choice, political contests attracted hundreds of voters. People packed the school auditoriums until not another human could get in and many stood in the hallways hoping to catch a few words. A gathering on the courthouse square brought out whole families and often an enterprising teenager peddled peanuts all around.

The soles on Woodrow's shoes took a beating during election time but personal door to door contact proved to be a valuable asset. Talking one-on-one to the farmers in Jay at the stock auction was imperative, too. People came from all over. Woodrow never knew if he was giving a political card to someone in Florida or Alabama. It didn't matter to him; they had friends all around.

On several occasions, Woodrow found himself making speeches from a donated flatbed truck—often without a loud speaker.

"My friends, my friends", he hollered trying to get the attention of a group at the county fair.

"Woodrow, here I am," responded one lonely voice in the crowd.

Others must have heard him because the results of the first primary proved that Woodrow did have supporters. He captured 1850 votes; Kimbrough got 1445 and West was eliminated with 945.

Morrison Kimbrough made a surprising announcement in the Press Gazette, May, 1946.

> *Mr. Kimbrough told the Gazette that he was sure Santa Rosa County would be well represented with Mr. Melvin as representative and in view of the fact that both their platforms were practically alike, he felt it foolish for the campaign to continue.*
>
> *"The farmers alone," Morrison said, "will save several thousand man hours of work which is badly needed in the fields by my getting out of the race. I do not believe the issues are worth this sacrifice."*

Woodrow ran unopposed in the November, 1946 election and in January, 1947 took his seat in the Florida House of Representatives as the rookie from Santa Rosa County. The average age of the members in the House was forty-five with fifty-seven of them college trained. Woodrow chided to a friend that he found his niche in a legislature predominated with thirty-eight lawyers.

Woodrow looked at his calendar and mentally tallied the

time he had to accomplish the task his voters expected of him—60 days. Since the Legislature met only once every two years, there was no time to dawdle. The first priority was to adopt a one-year budget then add ten percent for the second. For this complex and demanding process, legislators received six dollars a day plus ten three cent mailing stamps to cover the cost of communicating with their constituents. Frugal with the State's resources, Woodrow did not need all of his stamp allotment so he gave as many as eight or nine to the Miami delegation who sat in front of him.

Tom Beasley, speaker of the House of Representatives recognized Woodrow as highly qualified to serve on important committees such as agriculture, Salt Water Fisheries, Constitutional Amendments, Education and General Appropriations.

Having learned the value of a good education, Woodrow's deep concern for the students in Florida's educational system motivated him to work tirelessly on reform. As it was, every county in the state had multiple school districts. If it happened to be a rural area, sparsely populated, with little taxable property it was a poor district and the schools suffered from lack of funds; students did not receive the materials they needed.

"We've got to whittle these districts down to one per county," Woodrow argued to the committee, "and a decision must be made to tax wealth wherever it can be found in Florida and allocate it to the schools. We'll call this the Minimum Foundation Program. Now, I know it's not going to be popular with certain groups and no doubt it'll be an ongoing relentless battle to keep it funded properly but gentlemen, we have no choice; the students in our state are counting on us."

Opposition to the tax on state revenues reared its ugly head in his own county of Santa Rosa. Woodrow promised the voters, that if elected, he would introduce a special law equally dividing the race track money that all counties in Florida received between the Board of Public Instruction and the Board of County Commissioners. Since previously, all race track monies went into the Commissioner's treasury, several members vocalized their displeasure at a special meeting.

"How could Woodrow Melvin, the man we hired as our prosecuting attorney entertain such an idea? Has he forgotten who he's working for?" The chairman of the board's ire continued. "I make a motion we inform him immediately that if he follows through and insists on introducing this bill, his services will no longer be required. All in favor of sending a telegram to Tallahassee, vote by a show of hands."

Woodrow received the message the following day and chuckled as he read the words, "*services no longer required*".

"Well, this is going to work out good," he mused. "They can fire me if they want 'cause I've kept my word to the people; the bill passed with votes to spare this morning. I guess everybody's going to be happy."

It didn't take Woodrow long to figure out that sitting in the Legislature did not guarantee popularity among all of the members, especially if the bill did not coincide with everyone's thinking. Once again, Woodrow stood on his campaign promise of helping the farmers. Being an agricultural county, Santa Rosa farmers need tax relief on the fuel they put in their machinery. Determined to change the situation, Woodrow made a trip to Atlanta to confer with Georgia officials who already provided for a refund on gasoline provided for agriculture. Research indicated to him that Florida was one of seven states that taxed fuel in this manner.

The fur began to fly when Elgin Bayless, Chairman of the State Road Department, commented on the floor of the House, "Gasoline tax exemptions have proved to be failures in states where the policy has been tried. I predict that any attempt to exempt non-highway gasoline users from Florida's seven cent tax will lead to costly administrative programs and to such widespread abuses and evasions that the highway construction program will be endangered."

Woodrow stood his ground and argued, "There's an economic reason to pass such a bill. Farmers sell peanuts on the market and they have to compete with neighboring farmers in Alabama, Georgia and Mississippi who do receive rebates." The ensuing applause was encouraging but the Senate did not agree and no tax exemption for agriculture came out of the 1947 legislature.

Disappointed, Woodrow let it be known to all concerned that his fight to give farmers fuel tax relief would continue. Victory came in 1953 when the vote on the Senate floor was 19 to 16 in favor of a four-cent rebate.

Chapter Five
A Return to the House of Representatives

Readers of the Milton Gazette found in its premiere issue of 1948, a picture of a smiling cherub holding a large present marked *'My Wish for You'. Below it were the words. "Every new year is a sealed package ... as we start to unwrap 1948, it is my sincere hope that you are opening a big box of happiness."* Woodrow M. Melvin, Santa Rosa County Rep.

For Woodrow, 1948 started out on a political high. The news in the Gazette, February 5, was positive: "Woodrow Melvin, local attorney has been re-nominated to serve in the next session of the Florida legislature without opposition. This is the first time in many years that a representative has been elected in Santa Rosa County without an opponent. Melvin is recognized in Tallahassee as one of the state's outstanding legislators."

The summer of 1948 produced soaring temperatures but it was the heat generated by Harry S. Truman that threatened to split the Democratic party. Nominated in July at Convention Hall in Philadelphia, Pennsylvania, on a strong civil rights platform, this strategy found little favor with the southern delegates; especially, when Walter White, executive secretary of the National Association for the Advancement of Colored People, submitted a statement on behalf of twenty-one Negro organizations, declaring,

Party Must Decide

The day of reckoning has come when the Democratic party must decide whether it is going to permit bigots to dictate its philosophy and policy or whether the party can rise to the heights of Americanism which alone can justify its continued existence .We, therefore urge and insist that the platform of the Democratic convention endorse without equivocation the entire program of the President's committee on civil rights and especially those provisions to suppress lynching and mob violence, to ban the poll tax as a voting requirement, to afford equality of job opportunity and to abolish discrimination and segregation in the armed services, education and transportation.

A war of words, laced with echoes of history, blasted from the convention floor as the Northern delegates persuaded the majority to accept Truman's civil rights laws so strongly opposed in the South. The local Dixie sentiment published in the Gazette by the Democratic Executive Committee of Santa Rosa stated in a resolution,

"We commend the action of the Southern Governors and Southern Senators and Representatives in Congress for their opposition to President Truman's Civil Rights Program. We urge every true Democrat in Florida to repudiate it."

By 1994, Woodrow's attitude mellowed and remorse was evident when he explained the attitude of those times, "I'm not proud of it. Primarily, they were talking about school integration and registration to vote. In the south, to our eternal shame, there was a rigged registration. If a black person came in, they were given an examination they couldn't pass. It was called a literacy test but it was only applied to black people.

"Through the years, we came to realize that we are not going to have an equally staffed and trained school personnel for separate educational programs for the white and the black. We can't afford it financially; never have done it and the black schools traditionally have come up with the short end of the stick when there was a shortage of money. The idea of school desegregation was like a snowball coming down hill but the educational system in the south was not ready for it. In 1948, this county sure wasn't ready.

"It took Lyndon Johnson to get the Civil Rights legislated. He was a master at getting people to agree with him and told them what would happen if they didn't. There was a senator in Alabama who voted against him and a military operation was moved out of Alabama into Texas. They understood him—plain. There wasn't anything mysterious about what the man was saying. Johnson was really the power that moved Civil Rights into the forefront and changed the South's thinking."

1948 brought not only the Civil Rights issue, but financial storm clouds gathered and it looked as though state bankruptcy was on the horizon. The question on all of the legislators' minds was what would happen to the progress made in education, public health, and welfare during the previous session? Why was there a problem?

At the beginning of the 1949 legislative session, newly elected Fuller Warren issued a statement April 28, 1949 in an effort to explain the situation.

The public schools and colleges may not open in September. The old folks, dependent children, and the blind may not get their assistance checks. The insane asylum may have to send some of its inmates back home to their families.

I will tell you why. The 1947 legislature increased the State's contribution to public schools from $18,000,000 to $42,000,000 a year. It almost doubled *the appropriation for colleges. It greatly increased the appropriation for the old folks, dependent children and the blind .The 1947 legislature voted all these increases but it passed no taxes to pay for them. Many millions of dollars piled up in the treasury during the war when income from taxes was tremendous and the state was restricted from spending too much. The 1947 legislature wisely decided to use up all this war-accumulated surplus before voting any more taxes.*

During the past two years, the state spent a total of $33,000,000 more than was collected in taxes. The state treasury is almost dry and state comptroller, C.M. Gay, has told me that the treasury will be $3,000,000 in the red by September unless new or additional taxes are passed by the legislature .I propose that sufficient monies could come from businesses that make enormous profits in Florida but pay little or no taxes such as power and insurance companies, the hotel industry, and companies with out-of-state headquarters.

In no time at all, lobbyists of each of the interests concerned made their way to Tallahassee and paraded up and down the halls of the House bending the ears of every legislator willing to listen. Governor Warren was not impressed and became vocal:

These purchased protagonists have been doing their stuff day and night. In devious, deceptive ways these confusers for cash have been trying to throw dust in the eyes of the legislators.

To the governor's dismay, the legislature discarded the financial plan he'd proposed and now the only revenue in sight was the possibility of a general sales tax bill.

Woodrow sensed a crisis; both he and Governor Warren were elected on the promise that they would not support such a measure. After a few nights of lost sleep, Woodrow came to the conclusion that a sales tax had to be and they'd have to be honest with the voters.

At a special September 7 session, Woodrow volunteered to help write a face-saving bill and arranged with several other legislators to present it to Governor Warren.

"Governor, you said that you would veto a general sales tax; now, this is not a general sales tax because we are exempting food and medicine. So it is a special three percent sales tax."

The Governor's face brightened and his interest grew. "You've solved the problem, Woodrow. Thrown me a life-jacket. Is there anything else I need to know about the bill?"

"One more exemption, sir." A chuckle preceded the grin on Woodrow's face. "I believe we ought to exempt funeral expenses. My argument is that folks ought to die free and not get taxed on the way out."

A round of laughter concluded the meeting. "Have it on my desk for signature in the morning, gentlemen."

Woodrow, second from left, watches
Governor Fuller Warren sign a bill into law.

***

By 1950, Woodrow was a seasoned politician; he had two sessions in the House under his belt and looked forward to serving a third. Former County Commissioner, E.M. Fowler, saw things differently. As the deadline for candidates to qualify drew near, he tossed his hat into the representative race to oppose incumbent Melvin.

"Well, I'm back on the campaign trail, Nita," Woodrow announced at supper after reading Fowler's announcement in the paper.

His wife smiled and passed him the freshly baked cornbread. "Better eat up and take an extra one; as I recall, you missed a few meals on the last run for the House. Sure you're up to this?"

"Can't wait to start making speeches and shakin' every hand in the county, Nita. You know how I love to meet folks. Gotta get out there and hear what's on the public's mind."

David Melvin walked into his son's office March 30 with a copy of the Gazette under his arm.

"Look at this, Woodrow; you couldn't ask for a better endorsement. Have you read it yet?"

Woodrow looked up from the speech he was writing. "Haven't had time today, Dad. Read it to me."

A proud father read, "As a member of the legislature, Melvin is on the important education committee and is vice-chairman of the committee on appropriations. Melvin's outstanding work in the legislature has been in the promotion of better education. As a member of the Education Committee, he assisted in the writing and passage in 1947 of the Minimum Foundation Program that has brought the school program from the bottom of the ladder to its present place of top rank among the Southeastern states. He also passed a special bill for Santa Rosa County returning one-half of the county's share of race track money to the Board of Public Instruction."

A humble smile graced Woodrow's lips as he responded, "Just doin' what I was sent over there to do, Dad."

"Well, the talk I hear around Jay is mighty encouragin'."

"What are you hearing?"

"The Mayor's talked to the Jay Council about printing some sort of resolution concerning the support you've given them. Supposed to be in the Gazette this week; I'll be watching for it."

Sure enough, the March 23, issue contained the following

resolution.

Jay Council Thanks Melvin for Services:Representative
Given Appreciation for Outstanding Work

Whereas the special session of the1949 Florida
Legislature passed a law providing that the state tax on
cigarettes sold within a town shall be remitted by the
state to the town for any needed projects.

Whereas Woodrow M. Melvin, Representative of
Santa Rosa County did support this proposal, and
through his efforts the town of Jay will receive about
$4,600 each year and the town will be able to make
some needed improvements that will help all the citizens
of Jay.

Now, therefore, be it resolved by the mayor and the
town council of Jay, that the town of Jay, Florida, does
acknowledge and express its appreciation for the
faithful and unselfish service that has been performed by
Rep. Melvin for the benefit of all the people of Santa
Rosa County.

Be it further resolved that a copy of this resolution
be sent to Mr. Melvin, and also a copy to be sent to the
Gazette for publication.

H.V. Baxley, Mayor

The accolades drove home to the voters the truth of
Woodrow's commitment. September 14, readers opened the
Gazette to see yet another commendation.

Woodrow Melvin Is Recognized by 'Cracker Politics

The many friends and acquaintances of Woodrow
Melvin, Milton attorney and legislator, will be gratified
to note that his abilities and accomplishments are widely
recognized in Northwest Florida. An excerpt from a
recent political commentary declares that he has

39

"developed perhaps more rapidly in recent years than any other West Florida lawmaker.

Voters took that accolade to heart and returned their 'native son' to the House with a resounding victory over E.M. Fowler.

***

Only three days into the 1951 legislative session, Woodrow, along with five other men were appointed to escort the governor from his office to the House chambers. Although this was an honorary recognition, it was his appointment to the rules committee that carried the real weight since it drew the rules of procedure for the House and controlled the calendars.

Woodrow could not contain his excitement as he talked to his father by phone that night. "Dad, the rules and calendar is the power house; that's the one that determines whether your bill is even going to get on the calendar to be voted on or stays back in the cloakroom. I'm going to do my best to keep a full schedule to debate."

The Fresh Water Fish and Game Commission found that the old adage, 'You can take the boy out of the country but you can't take the country out of the boy', struck a childhood chord in Woodrow Melvin. They wanted a bill passed that required a one dollar annual license for Florida residents to fish in fresh water with cane poles in their home counties.

Memories of he and his brothers picking dew worms for bait and then slinging their poles over their shoulders and heading to the nearest creek to fish for bream encouraged Woodrow to stand up and voice his opinion to the House.

"We ought to have some activity in Florida the public can do free. If we tax the right of a man to fish in his own county, about the only thing he can do free is breathe air and drink water."

Woodrow breathed a sigh of relief when he heard the vote; 67 to 17 in favor of tax free pole fishing.

"I can't imagine," he mused, "the young lads in my county having to leave their poles on the porch all summer."

***

The 1951 session of the legislature brought with it rumblings and rumors of political corruption in Florida's government. Accusations of huge illegal campaign contributions made on behalf of Governor Warren surfaced and the word impeachment was on the lips of more than one legislator. A special committee headed up by Representative Haley of Sarasota began an investigation and the Sarasota Herald Tribune was quick to report:

> *William H. Johnston, C.V. Griffin and Lou Wolfson, who among them contributed more than $400,000 to Governor Warren's campaign, have been subpoened to appear before the Haley Committee here Saturday. Leo Edwards of Miami, chairman of the Florida Racing Commission, and B.P. Beville, secretary of the Racing Commission have also been asked to appear.*
>
> *Johnston, owner of four of Florida's nine dog racing tracks, Griffin, Howey-In-the Hills citrus operator and Wolfson, Jacksonville financier, have said under oath they each put more than $100,000 to the Warren campaign.*
>
> *Allegedly, the three met in Warren's office in Tallahassee shortly after his inauguration to "divvy" up state business. Warren has branded this statement false.*

Before the hearings began, to Woodrow's surprise, Haley presented him with a request.

"Woodrow, I've listened to you on the floor of the House and I like your straight-forward, direct approach. I need you to act as a counselor questioning the witnesses on behalf of my committee. We've got to get to the bottom of this mess before any time is wasted. Glenn Summers of Liberty County has agreed to work with you. What do you say?"

A moment of silence passed as Woodrow pondered the

41

question. *Here*, he thought, is *a challenge and an opportunity to sweep clean any corruption that may have reared its ugly head.*

"Tell Glenn to roll up his sleeves; we've got some work to do."

Burning the 'midnight oil', the two lawyers labored to come up with sharp, hard-hitting and probing questions that forced the facts out into the open and left the Racing Commission no choice but to clean house. Padded expense accounts, illegal use of public funds by the Commission and the reinstatement of bookmakers were all at the voters' disclosure.

Haley was jubilant and expressed his sentiment to Woodrow as he shook his hand in appreciation for a job well done.

"If the Miami 'boys' had previously never heard of Representative Woodrow Melvin from Santa Rosa County, they know you now."

Even the Miami Herald couldn't deny a superior effort made by Woodrow and Glenn to expose corruption in the Dog Racing arena as they stated May 7, 1951:

> *This capital city, buzzed over the weekend with talk of how the House committee to investigate corruption suddenly grew up from a sleepy kitten into a full-sized lion. They marveled at how legislator-counsel dug into the State Racing Commission in the sharpest and deepest probing ever seen around here.*
>
> *Another surprise was the way north and west Florida committee members, the "wool hat boys", Reps. Woodrow Melvin of way out in Milton, near the Alabama line, and Glenn Summers of Liberty County, had the racing commission on the ropes from the gong."*

Since there wasn't sufficient evidence to link Warren to corruption, no further move to impeach him was encouraged but the ordeal prompted both the House and the Senate to take a firm stand on political contributions given to candidates. The Senate was satisfied to curtail only contributions from race track interests but the House disagreed and once again Rep. Melvin stood his ground on the "No contributions amendment" he originated.

"The bill from the Senate does not go far enough; we desire not only the racing interests to get out of Florida politics, but the liquor interests and the utilities interests. I think the House ought not to kid itself about this legislation. The way to clean up politics is to block off those who make the major contributions to political campaigns. I'm not inclined to take any crumbs from the table that the Senate sends over."

In the final analysis, a bill passed that limited campaign contributions by any one person to $1000.

***

A man of fiscal responsibility, Woodrow did not forget that one of his campaign planks was to see that the public monies were used for their intended purpose and not wasted. Speaking to his peers in the House, he urged that departments should be called to strict account on their requests for additional money to carry on the same operations for the next two years that they conducted successfully for less in the last two.

"It is proper to ask 'why?' and 'where?' as to the salary and other expense increases. Let me enlighten you on some abuses that should be corrected.

"No one has yet suggested a good reason why the Motor Vehicle department needs special counsel at the rate of $500 a month; or the Beverage Department two attorneys at a rate of $916 a month; the Racing Commission, one attorney at $250 a month; the Real Estate Commission, two attorneys at $1400 a month, the State Board of Health at $400 a month or the State Welfare Board at $250 a month. The list goes on, gentlemen, and there is no reason for duplication of legal services. Many thousands of dollars could be saved by returning the state's legal business to the office of the attorney general, who is one of the most competent attorneys ever to serve in that capacity.

"The welfare budget calls for an increase of twenty-eight percent for salaries and thirty-five percent for 'other expenses' but only nine percent for old age assistance and twenty-seven percent for dependent children. A child can't help its situation and must be provided for. The primary responsibility for its support should be placed upon its father, who in many cases would be able to take care of the child if required to do so. The legislature will have before it for consideration proposed laws which will place the burden of support upon the one responsible for the situation.

"In conclusion, some may argue that these items are but mere 'drops in the bucket' but may I suggest to you that if the trend is allowed to continue and to grow, we may drop the bucket."

***

Always an advocate for better education, one of the most important tasks Woodrow accomplished during the 1951 session gained favor with Tom Bailey, the State Superintendent of Education, as he quoted, "Using a portion of car license tag money for school buildings and new equipment is one of the most constructive pieces of legislation enacted by the Florida Legislature in many years. There is no question that Representative Melvin proves to be a friend of the public schools. His interest in education, results not only in improved standards, but also opens a door of opportunity to higher learning."

At the completion of the 1951 legislative session, Woodrow Melvin represented the interests of his fellow constituents in the House of Representatives for three successive terms-1947,1949 and 1951. During this time, he concentrated his efforts on the advancement of education, welfare, and public health.

In his heart, he knew he'd given the best he could muster to the state. Was it time to turn his back on politics and return to Milton to practice law full time? The question haunted him for days until he made a decision. Woodrow had other plans.

Chapter Six
On to the Senate

By 1951, Woodrow's political gears were well greased; he knew his way through the legislative maze and his desire to work for the public still ignited his passion to help people. *This time*, he thought, *why not go for the Senate?*

In 1952, according to a special 'gentlemen's agreement', it was Santa Rosa's turn to provide a senator to represent both Okaloosa and Santa Rosa County. Ordinarily, the two counties alternated in sending a representative, however, in 1948 a special situation arose. Senator Bracken, from Okaloosa County was president of the senate and it was in the interest of both counties if he continued in that position for another term. Santa Rosa County agreed to withhold candidates on the condition that when the 1952 election came around Okaloosa would not support a candidate.

Woodrow no sooner qualified to run for state senator for District 1 when across the county line came a contender by the name of W.D. (Cooter) Douglas, a Crestview radio commentator. Woodrow smelled a rat and he was not shy about voicing his suspicion to the Milton Press Gazette on February 7,1952.

Melvin Repudiates Support Statement by Newman Brackin

State Representative Woodrow Melvin fired the opening salvo in his campaign for state senator here today by rejecting a declaration of support from incumbent Senator Newman Brackin of Crestview. In a strongly worded statement, Melvin virtually accused the former Senate president of sponsoring the candidacy of an Okaloosa County man for the post. Brackin himself is not a candidate for re-election to the senate position he's held for nearly eight years. The Crestview senator said in a public statement last week that he would uphold the "gentlemen's agreement" between Okaloosa and Santa Rosa counties by supporting a Santa Rosa man as his successor. Melvin is the only Santa Rosa County man in the race.

"Mr. Brackin has not fooled anyone by his statement that he will support a Santa Rosa County candidate," Mr. Melvin declared. "I am the only candidate in the race from Santa Rosa and I will repudiate Mr.Brackin's effort to mislead the people in this matter."

During the past session of legislature,"the Rep. explained, "I considered it my duty to oppose a proposed law by which Senator Brackin desired to create a third circuit judge in our judicial circuit. Judge L.L.Fabinski and Judge D. Stuart Gillis each advised me that they did not need the help of an additional judge." He continued, "I could see no good purpose to be served by putting the expense of an another judge on the people just to satisfy Newman Brackin's program. I view the Senator's statement with disgust. This is simply another instance when he has tried to talk out of both sides of his mouth at the same time. I had the opportunity to kill the proposed law and I did so in the face of Brackin's threat that he would see to it that I had opposition in my race for the senate."

The first round of the campaign ignited sparks in the public domain. To everyone's surprise, a letter of support, printed in the Press Gazette, February 14,1952, came from an Okaloosa resident.

Okaloosa Resident Regrets Violation of County's Pledge

Dear Editor,

I wish to express my sincere regret that an Okaloosan has seen fit to qualify as a candidate for the office of state senator in violation of the "Gentlemen's Agreement" of many years duration. I personally feel, along with many others that the citizens of Okaloosa County cannot afford to be placed in a position by any resident of this county where we are unwillingly forced to violate the sacred trust with the citizens of Santa Rosa County. Four years ago, the citizens of Santa Rosa County at the request of the citizens of Okaloosa County relinquished their right to nominate candidates for the senate. We agreed to return the favor by granting that county the privilege of nominees without opposition from this county for an equal period of time. It was assumed that all the Okaloosans sanctioned this agreement at the time since the honor favored this county. At least no one voiced any objection. The citizens of Santa Rosa County, in co-operation with our request, made a successful effort to prevent a nomination from that county.

We the citizens of Okaloosa County cannot afford to have our word of honor trampled upon in such a manner. Therefore, it is my hope that in some way the candidate could bring himself to withdraw from the race thus saving face for the people of this county who are so mortified over having our pledge to the people of Santa Rosa County broken.

Roger Pryor of Mary Esther

Douglas ignored the plea and continued to campaign despite the fact the records showed his own wife signed the "Gentlemen's Agreement" four years previously. The heat generated by the controversy drew swelling crowds at the first rally at Blackman on April 10,1952.

Nita straightened Woodrow's tie as he prepared to meet the public and whispered in his ear , "Thank goodness I have a husband who stands up for what his wife believes in. Go get him."

"I'm puttin' the gloves on for this one, my dear. Mr. Douglas and I are going to go a round or two."

Applause erupted from the crowd following the moderator's introduction of the candidates and then it was 'no holds barred' as the discussions began.

Douglas, eager to expound on his pledges began, "I promise to obtain bigger pensions for the old folks; they've worked hard and they deserve a whole lot more. Then there's the young folks. We send them off to war to fight for our country but we don't let them vote. It's not right, folks. You farmers out there will be happy to know I intend to eliminate the tax on gasoline for tractors and we need to do the same for fishing boats."

Woodrow looked at his opponent in amazement. *Does the man not have an original thought?* Every promise Douglas proposed Woodrow had initiated in the past sessions and had strived tirelessly to pass in the legislature.

Woodrow came to his own defense and he smiled at Douglas as he took over the debate.

"Mr. Douglas, I commend you on your ability to talk on the radio as a commentator but may I remind you that for the past three legislative sessions I've been talking on the floor of the House for the benefit of my constituents. The records show I helped pass through the House a bill that would have removed the tax from gasoline used in farm tractors but the bill died in the senate. My name is also on a constitutional amendment lowering the voting age to eighteen. It also died in the House. We need a senator who will fight for the people."

Woodrow was not finished and continued to inform his

opponent.

"Perhaps you'd like to know that the children in the state of Florida are better off today because of the Minimum Foundation School Law which I helped write and is strongly endorsed by the Santa Rosa County School Board, the Santa Rosa County Teachers' Association and the county's Principals' Association.

"I led a fight in the House that killed a bill that would have placed a lien on the property of those who received welfare grants. I will continue to work for increased assistance to the aged, blind and dependent children. Ladies and gentlemen, even if my opponent were elected, he couldn't make good his promise to eliminate welfare case workers. The manner in which the welfare program is conducted is determined by the Federal government. It's a matter over which a state senator can have no control."

Woodrow paused for a moment, looked Douglas straight in the eye and said, "Sir, let's bring this debate closer to home. If you will, let your memory take you back to the "Gentlemen's Agreement" between Santa Rosa County and Okaloosa County."

Douglas was quick to respond, "I signed no pledge to uphold the agreement."

"But the records indicate that your wife did. Am I correct?"

Heightened color crept up the side of Douglas's neck. "She may have; I'm not responsible for her actions."

A snicker ran through the audience then turned to applause as Woodrow fired back, "When my wife makes an obligation, you'll find me backing her up."

***

The election results on May 8, 1952 spoke volumes; Melvin walloped Douglas two-to-one with Melvin receiving 4,142 votes and Douglas getting 2,120.

Always thankful to his supporters, Woodrow placed an acknowledgement in the Press Gazette on May 15,1952.

To my friends and neighbors, thank you sincerely

for your vote and support in my race for the State Senate in District 1 which is composed of Santa Rosa and Okaloosa counties. I am deeply appreciative of the confidence you have placed in me. Mindful of my responsibilities to you, the people, I will constantly work to make you the best state senator our state has ever had.

Faithfully yours,
Woodrow Melvin

A week later, Nita greeted Woodrow home for supper with her usual kiss and handed him an envelope.

"The mailman delivered this today. Recognize the handwriting?"

Woodrow examined the script and shook his head. "Doesn't look familiar; let's take a look." He took a table knife, made a slice down the back of the envelope, and pulled out a sheet of paper. His eyes surveyed the content as his face broke into an impish grin and a hearty laugh rolled up from within.

"My goodness!" Nita said, "Let me see."

"Here," Woodrow handed his wife the paper. "Read it out loud."

After a brief glance, Nita did as he requested.

> I'm off to Tallahassee
> For to take my Senate seat.
> When I start shootin' off my mouth
> I'm mighty hard to beat.
>
> Oh, Susanna, Oh, don't you cry for me,
> I'm off for Tallahassee
> There's nowhere I'd rather be.
>
> I'm off for Tallahassee
> With my favorite at-te-che
> Don't know just what I'm gonna do

Or what I'm gonna say.

Oh, Susanna, Oh don't you cry for me.
I'm off for Tallahassee
With a cutie on my knee.

Anonymous

***

As each session of the legislature opened, Tallahassee experienced a temporary population explosion of more than senators and representatives sent by the people. Lobbyists crowded the hallways and vied for time with any committee member that would serve their interests.

The Sarasota Tribune, in an April 17, issue felt there was cause for concern.

> *At first glance, one is inclined to feel that Senator Carlton exaggerated in implying that only measures supported by lobbyists have a chance of being cleared by the state legislature. But on second thought, this inclination is weakened. Glancing back over the past several years, one recalls hearing recurrent reports of the growing number and power of lobbyists who gather at Tallahassee for each session of the legislature. Throughout, there were expressions of fear of the power and financial backing of the 'third house.' And it's easy to recall much legislation which, according to the opinion of the man in the street, could not have been passed but for the money and influence of the lobbyists.*
>
> *There is a list of more than eighty lobbyists who have registered for this session, with more to come. It could easily be that to an alarming extent we are being governed by lobbyist and not by the senators and representatives we send to Tallahassee.*

Sadly, two segments of the population, the deaf and blind

and the mentally ill could boast of no lobbyist stumping on their behalf. After an on-site inspection of the State Hospital at Chattahoochee, Woodrow came home disgruntled and upset.

"You had to see the facility and those desperate folks to believe the pitiful conditions they tolerate every day, Nita. Overcrowding, filth, too few medical personnel and the look of despair on the patients will haunt me forever." Woodrow pushed his half-eaten supper plate away. "Senators Carlton, Fraser and I are on a committee and I'll not rest until these facilities are brought up to acceptable standards."

"Sounds to me as though these dear folks have finally found their own lobbyists." Nita reached over and squeezed her husband's hand.

With a sigh, Woodrow responded, "I'll try; I know I won't sleep at night if I don't initiate some sort of reform."

Woodrow kept his word and according to The Tallahassee Democrat Newspaper, the 1953 session of the legislature was a productive one.

Legislature was Constructive

When we think back over the record of the 1953 session of the Florida Legislature, we have no trouble recalling a number of sound accomplishments and we find it difficult to think of even one serious defect in the bills enacted into law. That does not mean that the session was perfect. Some good bills were not passed; some bills that did pass could have been improved .It does mean that the Legislature left a fine record that it passed many good forward-looking measures and that the failures and mistakes were few and relatively unimportant. Here are some of the accomplishments:

1. Opening the welfare rolls to public inspection.

2. Authorizing a trial run on the toll turnpike idea.

3. An extra tax on dog tracks to help each county and to put the physically handicapped on the welfare rolls.

4. Adding to consumer representation on the price-fixing milk board.

5. Providing funds to advance education, health, pest control, custodial care, establish a state medical school and a new mental hospital.

That's not at all a bad record of accomplishments for one session. We think Governor Dan McCarty spoke the truth when he told the Legislature that it worked hard and accomplished much."

***

A top senatorial position awaited Woodrow on his return to the 1955 Florida Legislature.

Two special bills, which applied directly to Santa Rosa County, were introduced by Senator Melvin and passed the Senate.

The first took certain powers away from the County Commissioners. In the past, the positions of county attorney and prosecuting attorney were appointments. In the future, the people of the county would elect a candidate to act not only as county attorney but also prosecuting attorney, attorney for the Board of Commissioners, the Board of Public Instruction and the Santa Rosa Island Authority.

Continuing the fight for educational funding, Woodrow wrote the second bill which required the County Commissioners to pay over to the Board of Public Instruction, the first $50,000 and half of all remaining monies received by the county from race track revenue.

The 1955 session took off in Woodrow's favor but it wasn't long before he found himself at odds with Governor Collins; the reapportionment of the number of senators for the state was a hot issue. Southern Florida wanted more control in the legislature at the expense of northern Florida. Woodrow didn't agree and his vocal protests attracted attention from his opponents.

He argued, *"Instead of threatening to punish the people*

living in certain Senate districts in order to coerce votes in the Legislature, the Road Department could render a real service to all the people in Florida if it would now put a stop to the practice of awarding road contracts to those favored few contractors who are now delinquent on contracts and can't possibly get the work done in a reasonable length of time."

This salvo struck a nerve with Road Board member, Al Rogero of Clearwater who retaliated, *"Senator Melvin, I suggest that Governor Collins withhold road building money from districts represented by senators who oppose reapportioning the Senate along lines recommended by him."*

This confrontation, prompted Woodrow to hold a conference with a group of Santa Rosa political leaders in which he stated, *"Gentlemen, this man means business; Rogero is threatening legislators and 'specially anointed contractor-disciples' are growing fat and mighty at the Road 'pork barrel'. If the Road Department would push these contractors away, while the people wait in vain for their roads to be built, the public would gain confidence that their interests are being heard.*

"I'm concerned that Santa Rosa and Okaloosa Counties will be cut off, along with others, because I haven't voted on a bill in the legislature as the governor would have me vote. He wants one senator each for Bay, Monroe, Manatee and Sarasota counties. I and other opponents of the plan are willing to give senators to Bay and Monroe. Now, I'm not opposed to giving Sarasota a senator if Okaloosa, which is nearly as populous, were given one, too.

"On two separate occasions, a majority of the one-hundred and thirty-three members of the Legislature has passed a reapportionment law on the basis of population. Twice the governor has rejected and vetoed our efforts demanding each time a law containing provisions as he desires. The people in the First Senatorial District did not elect me to serve in the Senate as a rubber stamp for any governor, or of any member of the Road Department who might speak for the governor."

A hearty round of applause followed by a declaration of support from the School Board Chairman boosted Woodrow's morale. "Don't let these fat cats intimidate our county. We're standing right beside you."

Woodrow ontinued, "Reapportioning the Senate as suggested by Governor Collins would give the large county blocs a majority and endanger the present distribution of state funds. Our present laws concerning distribution of race track funds, educational funds, gasoline taxes, and cigarette tax to our towns, are eminently fair and reasonable. They provide benefits to all our state. I, and many other senators and members of the house, have publicly expressed the fear that if the time ever came when a limited area in the state obtained voting control in both branches of the legislature, the distribution of those funds could be changed; we'd be in danger of losing them."

The Chairman of the Democratic Party spoke up, "You've worked too hard over these past several years to lose all those gains, Woodrow. Go back over there and stand your ground."

A week later, the ringing telephone caught Woodrow's attention as he walked into his Tallahassee office. A secretary motioned that the call was for him.

"Hello."

"Woodrow, it's Perry."

"Hey, brother, what's up? Good to hear from you."

"Have you seen a paper this morning?"

"Just walked in the office—anything new?"

"You're going to love this, Woodrow; the Miami Herald isn't too happy with you fellows from northwest Florida. They've coined a new title -- The Pork Chop Gang."

Woodrow's body shook with laughter while Perry continued, "Seems like the senators from Orlando, Tampa, Fort Lauderdale and Miami don't like the idea that they only have eighteen votes in the senate and northwest Florida has twenty."

"Too bad," Woodrow replied. "We weren't the ones who set up the voting; that was a result of earlier politics. I know the population is moving south and they want more of the thirty-eight votes and believe it or not, brother, I see the merit in that, but you know, you don't give somebody a stick and then ask them not to hit you with it. We're not giving them anymore votes."

Perry chuckled, "That's my brother. So you don't mind the fact that they think northwest Florida is made up of nothing more than pine trees, poultry and swine?"

"I believe we'll wear it with pride. Thanks for the 'heads up', Perry. Take care."

***

On the final day of the 1955 legislative session, Woodrow, one of the last senators to leave the Senate Chamber, picked up his briefcase, and surveyed the historical room with its blue and white décor, twenty-two foot ceiling and cresent-shaped rows of oak desks. A lump lodged in Woodrow's throat as he realized his time in the legislature to serve the people of North West Florida was over.

A sigh of resignation led him to ponder, *"Did I deliver to the voters as best I could on the platform promises? How many speeches did they hear through bullhorns, microphones and radio broadcasts? Did those long hours of drafting, rewriting and debating over a bill whether it be on the floor of the House, Senate or in a smoke-filled room at the Floridan Hotel make a difference in the life of the average man, woman or child in our "Sunshine" state? I guess history will be my judge."*

Members of the Florida Senate;:
Woodrow is standing in the bottom row,
third from the right.

Part Two

Chapter Seven
Judicial Years

Of all the legislation passed during the 1955 Legislative session, one bill affected no one man in Okaloosa, Santa Rosa, Escambia, and Walton counties as personally as it did Woodrow Melvin. Because of the rapid growth in these counties, an additional judgeship was needed for the First Judicial Circuit. Once again, an opportunity to serve in public life tempted him to submit the paperwork that qualified him as a candidate.

As the filing date grew closer, Nita noted one morning at breakfast that her husband was not his usual self. "Woodrow, more coffee?"

She received no reply and a quick glance in his direction told her that the question fell on deaf ears. Woodrow's eyes stared out the kitchen window at Blackwater Bay.

"Woodrow, you were restless in your sleep last night and this morning you seem self-absorbed. Is something bothering you that we haven't discussed?"

Woodrow gave his wife that familiar grin she knew preceded a confession.

"Sorry, honey, I've been wrestling with this idea to run for the circuit court judge in our district. But my interests are not the only ones to consider. My primary consideration is for our family; five young children need their daddy home and during the past few years, I've spent a good deal of time in Tallahassee. Being a judge means traveling from one circuit court to another."

Nita poured him another cup of coffee, took the seat next to him at the table and looked him straight in the eye.

"Listen to me Woodrow Melvin; since the day you passed your bar exam, I know it's been a longing of yours to sit on the bench. Your opportunity has come and I'll be the last person to stand in your way. You know I can handle the responsibilities on the home front."

Woodrow took her hand in his and squeezed it in affirmation. "And I'm so fortunate and thankful to have a wife who shares my dream. But how do you feel about me having to put my law practice aside? We'll be eating hamburger instead of steak; going from $30,000 a year down to $10,000. In fact, I helped to write the amendment to the Appropriation Act. It's going to increase to $12,500 but the constitution states that if a member of the legislature votes to increase the emoluments of an office, they're not entitled to receive increased compensation for two years."

The smile on Nita's face lifted the burden he carried.

"How do you like your hamburger cooked, Judge Melvin?"

***

On January 9, 1957, gusts of cold, damp wind swept across the Gulf of Mexico and blew along the streets of Pensacola, Florida, right up to the doors of the Escambia County Court-house. Although the air outside was bone-chilling, the atmosphere inside the building was warm and welcoming. Family, friends, attorneys, reporters and judges gathered to witness Woodrow receive his oath of office as circuit court judge for District 1 from Record Court Judge Ernest E. Mason and Judge Harold B. Crosby. At age forty-four, Woodrow knew his responsibilities would challenge his knowledge of the law and put his character on the altar of a scrutinizing public. This time, instead of helping to write the laws, his job was to interrupt them within the framework of the Constitution—nothing more; nothing less.

Following the Pledge of Allegiance, Woodrow, calm and with a sense of reverence, stepped in front of the bench and faced Judge Crosby.

Before he administered the oath, Judge Crosby instructed his charge, "A judge should not allow other affairs or his private interests to interfere with the prompt and proper performance of his judicial duties. An independent judiciary presupposes the existence of two conditions. First, your position is free from the legislative or executive branches of government and secondly, you must be willing to restrain yourself from attempting to exercise powers that are properly legislative in nature."

Woodrow nodded in agreement and Judge Crosby continued, "Portions of the charge for judges is found in the Scriptures when it says, "And I charged your judges at that time, saying hear the causes between your brethren, and judge righteously between every man and his brother, and the stranger that is with him. Ye shall not respect persons in judgment; but ye shall hear the small as well as the great."

Judge Crosby cleared his throat, looked into Woodrow's face and said, "Repeat this oath after me."

Woodrow straightened his shoulders, took a deep breath and repeated each line.

"*I, Woodrow Maxwell Melvin, do solemnly swear that I will administer justice without respect to persons, and do equal right to the poor and to the rich and that I will faithfully and impartially discharge and perform all the duties incumbent upon me as Woodrow Maxwell Melvin under the Constitution and laws of the United States. So help me God.*"

Right on cue, Nita stepped forward with tears spilling onto her cheeks and slipped the black robe around her husband's shoulders.

"Judge Melvin, come take your place on the bench," commanded Judge Crosby as everyone broke into applause.

No stranger to public speaking, Woodrow responded, "I'm proud to be a lawyer and now a judge; I pray I may always remember I am a lawyer."

Without hesitation, Woodrow continued his acceptance speech.

"The framers of our Constitution wisely decided there shall be three separate and distinct branches of government. The legislative branch was given the prerogative of writing laws. The responsibility for enforcement was placed in the hands of the executive department. The sole responsibility of the judiciary is interpretation. It is regrettable there are those judges who have assumed the responsibility to take their pens to sign decrees to make laws which were never voted by the legislative branch or to amend a constitution without the vote of the people as intended. Maintaining the three branches of our government as originally intended provides the last fond hope of a free people that a democracy shall not perish from the earth."

Woodrow let his eyes take in the gathering intent on hearing his words and closed with a prayer. *"Forever in this court give tongue to those who plead for the oppressed, who would whisper words of encouragement to the despairing, who work for justice and promote peace and harmony among our citizens."*

Another day in court for Judge Melvin

62

The oath of office is administered by
Judge Melvin to school board members.

Circuit Court Judges
Woodrow is third from left

Chapter Eight
Lillian's Story

"You've been a judge a mere eighteen days and already your name is in the paper," Nita teased as Woodrow placed a stack of folders into his brief case and snapped the lid shut. "And not just in the Press Gazette—the story comes out of New York."

"What in tarnation did I do now?" Woodrow bent over his wife's shoulder to scan the newspaper she spread out on the table.

"Ljerka arrived from Yugoslavia yesterday. Isn't that wonderful! And you made it happen, Woodrow."

"No, no; I was simply a backstage worker. Senator Smathers is the main player in this story."

Nita drew in a deep breath and prepared for a debate. "I'm giving credit where credit is due, my dear husband. If you hadn't taken the ball and run with it to Senator Smathers that little girl would still be over yonder sitting in an orphanage. Here, read the article for yourself."

Woodrow's eyes followed Nita's hand to the bold, black letters and silently read:

Milton Resident: Woman, Daughter Finally United

A woman from Milton, Florida and the daughter

whom she had not seen for four years had a tearful reunion today when the girl arrived from their native Yugoslavia.

Mrs. Gloria Placek, widowed operator of the Red River Range Motel, was on hand at International Airport when her eleven –year-old daughter, Ljerka Zagar, who had been living in a children's home in Zagreb, Yugoslavia, arrived on a plane from Vienna.

They instantly recognized each other. They rushed forward and embraced and Mrs. Placek began to cry. As she patted the child's face, she asked in her native tongue, "How do you feel? What kind of trip did you have?"

The girl, who appeared shy and was obviously tired from the twenty-four hour journey from Zagreb, said, "It was long."

The mother and daughter were separated when Mrs. Placek was unable to obtain a visa for the child before her departure from Zagreb in October, 1952.

Mrs. Placek praised Judge Woodrow Melvin of Milton and Senator George Smathers who worked to obtain a special dispensation to facilitate Ljerka's entry into the United States.

Woodrow wiped away a tear as he folded the newspaper.

"What a great way to start the day. Gloria's ordeal is finally over. We'll have to welcome this little girl in a big way, Nita. We'll plan a party."

Placing a kiss on his wife's cheek as he prepared to leave, Woodrow asked, "Could you bake a fancy cake, honey?"

"Chocolate or vanilla?"

"Chocolate, of course—my favorite."

***

Milton embraced their newest resident with a grand celebration. As Gloria and Ljerka stepped from the train, the

66

Mayor, surrounded by a cheering crowd, placed a bouquet of roses in the little girl's arms.

"Smile for the camera, sweetie," called out a reporter as he took one photo after another.

Overwhelmed by the attention, Ljerka clung to her mother until Woodrow, with his friendly, comforting smile, walked over and introduced himself along with Nita and their children. Before long, Ljerka relaxed and when her mother asked if she was ready to go to a party, her eyes sparkled and she nodded in agreement.

Guests seated themselves on the grounds of Woodrow and Nita's home as water from Blackwater Bay lapped against the shore. Everyone's ears perked up when Woodrow asked Gloria to tell her story.

"I was born in Yugoslavia. My mother died when my brother and I were very young. We were taken in to live with my aunt and uncle who wanted to come to the United States but it was the beginning of the war and we could go nowhere. So we wait until things quiet down; meantime, things change. My brother died, I got married and had a little girl. But I divorced my husband and in 1950, decided to work on my papers to come to the States. Two years later, I arrived in America. I could not bring Ljerka at that time because her father would have stopped me. It was easier for me to come first and then work on the papers to bring her. As soon as he found out I had left, he put Ljerka in an orphanage.

"I lived with foster parents until I married Joe Placek and we moved to Milton where we bought the Red River Range Motel. My husband wanted to adopt Ljerka so he went to find someone to help with the paperwork. Mr. Johnson recommended Woodrow Melvin. Before the papers were finished, my husband dropped dead of a heart attack. I was four and a half months pregnant and had a little girl in Yugoslavia."

Gloria's voice trembled and she paused, took a sip of water then continued, "Because my husband was a United States citizen and I was not, all papers went into the trash. I have to start all over again so I asked Mr. Melvin to help me. He told me to wait and he would see what could be done. Meanwhile, he got in touch with Senator George Smathers in Washington, D.C."

Gloria glanced at Woodrow and smiled in appreciation.

"Because Ljerka was over ten years old, she could not automatically come and that is why we have trouble. In Washington, the Senators had a meeting and they passed a special law that Ljerka can come over here before the two- and- a –quarter- year waiting period. Many calls and telegrams were sent from Judge Melvin's office and investigators from the immigration came to see me and wanted to know the special reason I was asking for help. I just told them my situation. But, Judge Melvin was the main one pushing and pulling on all sides. He had really good success."

Applause erupted from the guests then all eyes returned to Gloria.

"Yesterday was so exciting; I met her in New York." Tears glistened on Gloria's cheeks as she reached for her daughter. "It was four long years since I'd seen her. The Red Cross put her on the plane. They pinned a label on her coat—front and back with her name and mine. She recognized me right away."

Gloria directed her gaze at Woodrow as she concluded, "Judge Melvin, you were sent from God. Without your help, I would have had to wait over two years for Ljerka. You are like a father to me; thank you, thank you."

Woodrow stepped forward to give further explanation of the situation.

"Senator Smathers happens to be a personal friend of mine and he has a heart as big as all outdoors. I played a secondary role in all of this. When he understood the problem, he put an amendment on the annual appropriation bill simply naming this child and directing that a visa be issued to her without regard to quotas. Just issue a visa with clearance to apply for citizenship. No special privileges; she'll have to take the examination like everyone else.

"The legislative process in congress is so different than it is in the states. In Florida, you can't do that. If you wanted to put an amendment on an appropriation act, the subject matter would have to relate to appropriations. In congress, it can relate to anything in God's world. That's how it was done; it was simply a provision and they were directed to do it.

"I'd like to give credit to the Yugoslavia State Department, too. They wrote a letter wanting to know about the financial responsibility of the step-father. Unfortunately, he died before this thing was over. But they weren't going to permit a citizen of Yugoslavia to come here unless they were satisfied as well as we were. So we got a certified public accountant to prepare a statement as to the assets he left and then Yugoslavia was ready to grant Ljerka a visa to leave. Senator Smathers worked it all out; he was the brains behind it."

Another round of applause preceded Woodrow's announcement.

"Enough speeches; let's eat! Nita where's that chocolate cake?"

***

The Melvin residence, full of laughter, love, tears and childhood activity became a second home to Ljerka, who changed her name to Lillian. She and Laura, Woodrow and Nita's daughter, spent many hours scavaging the Blackwater Bay shoreline for anything the tide brought within their reach. Giggles and girl talk filled the air as their imaginations went wild.

"Maybe we'll find one of those bottles with a message in it, Lillian," Laura's words hinted at suspense. "It could say, "Help come save me. I'm on an island all alone.""

Lillian's carefree expression changed and she grew pensive as she stopped walking and looked out over the horizon.

"I felt all alone once, Laura. When I was in Yugoslavia."

"But why? You lived with your father and grandmother didn't you?"

"Not for long; my father took me to an orphanage when I was seven. He worked nights and I guess he thought I was too much trouble for my grandmother. She was very old."

The girls sauntered up to a beached log and sat down as Lillian continued, "I missed my family, especially with mother here in Florida , so I'd run away and go back to Father. I pleaded

69

with him to let me stay but he always found a different orphanage."

Laura couldn't contain her curiosity and she pressed forward with her questions.

"Were they mean to you?"

"Not the last one; some of the ladies liked me and would even take me home with them. I liked that because then I could do the things Grandma taught me. In the Communist orphanage I was not allowed to do the things I was taught in my family."

"Like what?" Laura asked.

"Read the little booklets Grandma gave me and go to church with her. What family teaches you is all you know."

Laura nodded in agreement.

A tremor rippled through Lillian's voice and she wiped away a tear.

"Grandma died while I was in the last orphanage. It was built on a hill over-looking the city and you could look down and see the cemetery. I would stand at the window and see a light. One of the women put it there so I could see where she was buried."

"That was really sweet of her, Lillian. I bet that made you feel better."

"A little; but I missed my mother so much-- even more after Grandma died. Mama told me she'd send for me and every day I prayed she would. Then it happened."

Lillian paused to splash water on her reddening arms before continuing, "The head of the orphanage asked me if I wanted to stay there until I was eighteen..."

"Eighteen!" interrupted Laura. "Seven more years. Wow!"

"Or," Lillian continued, "come to America. He showed me a map of Florida."

"Did he really think you'd want to stay?"

"Some girls stayed. They had nowhere else to go."

"Oh, that's so sad. I'm happy you're with your mother now."

"Me too. But it hasn't been easy, Laura. So many things are different here—every day I learn new English words. School's not the same." Lillian snickered, "Mama says I even have to learn to eat grits and greens."

"Won't hurt you, girl. That's what'll make you one of us."

Lillian's young eyes looked into her friend's and she said, "I do feel like part of your family, Laura. I thank God for your father, Judge Melvin."

Chapter Nine
Grand Jury Respect

A hush came over the eighteen men assembled in the Santa Rosa County Court jury box as Judge Melvin took his seat on the bench.

"Good morning, Gentlemen."

A repetition of 'Morning, sir,' was followed by a smile or a nod of a head from each member.

Woodrow went right to business.

"As citizens of the United States of America, you have been called upon to serve on a Grand Jury. With this charge, comes a serious responsibility. Your oath means that no personal relationship is to be considered; that nothing be done from political motives. No man is to be presented for envy, hatred, or malice. In my opinion, there is no greater deterrent to evil and corruption than the inquiring mind and searching eye of a Grand Jury."

Sitting in the back of the courtroom, Tom Leonard, editor of the Press Gazette, listened and took notes as Woodrow explained the purpose of this court appointed jury. The following day, the residents of Milton read Leonard's commentary in the paper.

The grand jury serves a unique and useful part in

the government of our land. We have seen many instances in the past ten years in which the grand jury has used its investigative powers to ferret out information leading to definite recommendations for the betterment of the county. It is not always necessary to indict anyone to bring about amelioration of wrong-doing. Often the mere fact that the scrutiny of eighteen good and conscientious men are turned onto a bad situation is sufficient to mend their ways.

We appreciate the importance which our courts attach to the grand jury. We feel that the grand jury serves the same ends which we in the newspaper profession seek to serve. We do not, of course, have the power to subpoena and demand answers under oath. Neither do we have the deliberate benefits of eighteen of our peers to guide us. However, we do attempt to turn the light of information into the public life of our community. That light is intensified and focused by the grand jury.

Not everyone shared Woodrow or Leonard's respect for a grand jury. The personal safety of Russell Sloan, a sworn member, signed an affidavit stating that on June 22, 1958, he was sitting in the City Grill and Cecil Herndon came in the side door of the café and Ben Hall entered through the front door. Cecil walked behind Russell, leaned across the juke box for a moment then walked over to the table where Russell was sitting drinking a cola.

Cecil stated, "You're one of them guys on the grand jury."

Before Russell could answer, Herndon proceeded to repeatedly strike him in the face with his fist. Hall took one look at the blood gushing from Russell's nose and mouth and yelled, " C'mon, let's go."

Patrons rushed to the injured man's aid as a waitress called the police.

Quick to respond, the deputies listened to Don Penrod, owner of the café, "I saw the shorter one, Hall, look at Herndon and point to Russell. Next thing I seen was a big ole fist landing on that poor man's jaw. Herndon's at least a hundred pounds heavier; Russell never had a chance to defend himself. Go get'em boys."

Woodrow did not take the news lightly; he felt it was more than an assault on a fellow human being; it was an assault on the democratic process and he intended to see that the assailants got the message. He immediately issued an order for the arrest of the two men and he set the bail bond high--$2500 each.

Once again, Woodrow found support from the editor's June 25, 1959, opinion section in the Press Gazette.

> *At the opening of the spring term of Circuit Court, we had an editorial on the value of the Grand Jury in a democracy. We quoted freely from Judge Melvin's charge to the Grand Jury in which he set forth his convictions of the need for such a body and what he thought its purpose should be. We now have pending a hearing on a complaint by a member of the Santa Rosa County Grand Jury who was allegedly assaulted.*
>
> *It is heinous enough for a man to be brutally assaulted without personal provocation in a public place, regardless of the implications of his grand jury membership. We shall not dwell upon those implications, because we are well aware of the feelings of the judge as to the dignity and inviolability of this court-appointed body of men."*
>
> *Every citizen needs reassurance as to the individual's rights of peaceful existence when there has been as much violence as we have seen hereabouts recently. Further grand juries, during Judge Melvin's tenure of office will know they have the full support of the court behind them.*

Chapter Ten
Passion for the Law

"Why that's wonderful news, Woodrow!" Nita clapped her hands and kissed him on his cheek. "The law is certainly an old love of yours and who better to explain it to this generation than you. When do you start?"

"The spring semester at Pensacola Junior College starts a week after Easter this year so I have a couple weeks to prepare. It's an evening course so there's no conflict with my judicial duties." A smile curled around Woodrow's lips and his eyes sparkled. "Kinda lookin' forward to some lively debate with these young folk. Now that we've started the seventies decade, there's so much social change with the Vietnam war, attitudes toward the law are a whole lot different than when I was in college."

As Woodrow walked into the classroom days later, he noted several differences as his eyes scanned the twenty male and female students sitting in front of him. No longer were shirt and tie the attire for the men but multi-colored, tie-dyed tee shirts and blue jeans were worn by many of the males. At times, Woodrow had to scrutinize a student's body for gender clues since most of the class wore long hair. But one thing had not changed—with pens poised, the desire to learn warmed Woodrow's heart.

He began his lecture by holding up a copy of a newspaper. "Who read today's editorial in the Press Gazette?"

Three students raised their hands.

"Since this is a course in the fundamentals of law, I believe this article is a good place to start. For those of you who missed it, bear with me as I read."

Law Day

Saturday, May1, 1971, is Law Day, and we do not recall a time in America needed more stringently to be reminded of our heritage of law than today when lawlessness is rampant and the crime wave is growing in volume and heinousness. To quote from a Bar Association release:

The law, like the sun and rain, is for all of us.
Protect it. He who flouts it mocks you and steals your child's future.
Serve it. He who defies the law is rejected, but he who serves it is honored.
Give jury service in your community, assist and respect law enforcement officials, give court testimony when required.
Remember, the law is your protection.

At once, a young man in the second row raised his hand to get Woodrow's attention.

"Yes," Woodrow nodded toward him.

"Judge Melvin, sir, what makes you so passionate toward the law? I see breakdown and disrespect for law from the top of our society to the bottom—like the war protests, Watergate, crime."

Woodrow's eyes softened and a reflective smile proceeded his reply.

"Son, I've had a love affair with the law since I sat in a classroom, just like you, over forty years ago. This is one affair my wife encourages me to participate in."

A trickle of laughter circled the room before Woodrow continued, "Understand that the United States of America is one of the few countries in the world founded on a check and balance between the legislative, executive and judicial branches. I think they so balanced the structures of government because they knew that absolute power vested in any man corrupts absolutely. Each branch of government is co-equal with the other and as a result, no one branch can say to the other, "We have no need of you." In my opinion, the Constitution of our county is a work of pure genius. I am honored to be part of the process that makes it work."

A voice from the back of the room asked, "Why don't other countries use our system?"

"Power and greed," announced a girl taking notes.

Woodrow chimed in, "She's right; take Russia for example. For many years, each May 1st has been the day when the Red Square in Moscow turned into a military review field. There before the Premier and Bosses of the Kremlin, and the flag-waving, cheering throngs, the very latest in Russia's military might paraded –tanks, missiles, and guns. All done in honor of the military power of that government under Communist rule. Tune into the news and I'm sure you'll see what they want the world to see.

"Now, in contrast to that type of display, President D. Eisenhower issued a proclamation designating May1, 1958, as Law Day U.S.A. and the Joint Resolution of Congress designated Law Day as a special day of celebration by the American people in appreciation of their liberties and as an occasion for our re-dedication to the ideals of equality and justice under the Law."

"But Judge Melvin, I've never heard of it," said a black girl thumbing through her book. "Is it like a holiday for lawyers and judges?"

"No, we work May 1 just like everyone else; but you know, I almost wish Congress had declared it a holiday then folks would take notice of it. Remember this ladies and gentlemen, law and raw arbitrary power are in eternal enmity."

There was a moment of silence as Woodrow let his words penetrate the minds of his inquisitive students. Finally, he said, "Ready to delve deeper or do you need a break?"

A chorus of "continue" warmed his heart and he prepared to peel back another layer of his favorite subject matter.

"In totalitarian countries, there is a unique system they call justice under the name of 'People's Tribunal'—the direct participation of people in the judgment of their fellow citizens. The Communists call this 'Democratic Justice' and it can be traced back to Socrates. He addressed his accusers before a court that was composed of all the citizenry of Athens and described them as a multitude. Socrates had an uneasy feeling about the type of justice that would be administered by this group even in the highly civilized society of Athens. As the defendant, he spoke to the crowd, "I tell you the truth, no man who honestly strives against lawlessness and unrighteous deeds, and who opposes you or any other multitude, can save his life."

Woodrow put down his law book and opened his briefcase. He drew out a Bible, holding it up for all to view.

"Just curious," he asked, "but how many of you have read this book?"

A sprinkling of half-raised arms appeared around the class.

"One of the best cases for mob justice is found in The Gospels--Mark is a good example. Four centuries after Socrates dealt with the multitude in Athens, another people's tribunal convened in the Roman providence of Judea to pronounce judgment on a Galilean named Jesus."

A couple of students started nodding their head in agreement as they realized they knew the story Woodrow related. The others listened with rapt attention.

"In the Roman Empire of those days, the many communities of races and religions which it embraced were given a certain amount of home-rule. So it was with the Jewish community in Judea. Their judges, called high priests, came from their own members. Jesus, a Jew, went about this community as a teacher expounding unorthodox religious views. This did not go over well with the priests. They seized him and judged him guilty of blasphemy but the jurisdiction of the priestly court did not extend to inflicting corporal punishment. However, the priesthood was not satisfied simply to excommunicate Jesus; it was bent on eliminating him altogether. But they had a problem. Can anyone suggest what it was?"

The ticking of the clock was the only sound heard as the students pondered the question. Finally, a deep voice heard from a male in the third row broke the silence.

"I studied world history last semester and, throughout the Roman Empire, Rome decided who lived or died. The Jews had no civil authority; the death sentence had to come from a Roman in command."

Woodrow smiled and gave the lad a hand. "I hope you got an A on that course, son, because you're correct. Roman law could not condemn a Jew for blasphemy—only a crime against the state. That's why the religious authorities included in their indictment of Jesus that he called himself the 'King of the Jews', implying treason against Caesar.

A girl with braided blond hair shook her head and said, "Sounds like Jesus was framed."

Woodrow's face grew grim. "It gets worse than that. When he was summoned before the Governor, Pontius Pilate, along with a bandit named Barrabas, a great crowd hostile to Jesus thronged the trial. Pilate, found him not guilty—wanted to wash his hands of the whole affair but politics be as they may, he feared if he offended the Jewish leaders there'd be a riot in the streets of Jerusalem. To play it safe, he asked the crowd which prisoner they wanted released and the resounding answer was Barrabas. That still left the question of what to do with Jesus. Again Pilate took the easy way out. The crowd pronounced the fate of Jesus—"Crucify him!"

Woodrow was certain he heard a sniffle from the girl with the braid.

"Pilate let the crowd determine the judgment and sentence to be imposed against Jesus. This is the first time in history that a man who had been tried and found 'not guilty' was condemned to death by a judge. Mob justice, students, is the lowest form of justice. The words of Jesus hanging on the cross should haunt mankind forever, 'Father, forgive them; for they know not what they do.'

"To wrap things up for tonight, I think there is some significance to be attached to the fact that in writing our Constitution, one of the first purposes designated was to 'establish justice'. That purpose was placed ahead of providing for the common defense and promoting the general welfare. And for good reason. For if justice falls into disrepute and order depends upon the temper of the mob, neither defense, welfare, nor liberty can long endure."

Woodrow stopped talking and he let the students catch up with their note taking before he brought the session to a close.

"I hope you've gained some appreciation for the law this evening. Tomorrow is May 1st. Think about its importance; and," he paused before a sliver of a smile spread across his lips, "for those of you who haven't read Mark, do so. He tells the story a whole lot better than I did."

***

College students were not the only segment of the population eager to hear Woodrow's opinion and interpretation of the law. After an address to the Chamber of Commerce, January 25,1973, the editor of the Gazette commented, "When Judge Melvin talks, people listen. He never encumbers his speech with jokes or trivialities; he gets to the "meat" of what he has to say in a hurry and pounds home his points in an unobtrusive fashion."

Woodrow's speech to the Chamber of Commerce members began, "There is a voice in the soul of every human being that cries out for justice and freedom. Justice and freedom under law is America's answer to that voice.

" Though freedom and justice under law comes to you and me as a gift, yet it is not free. It carries with it a great responsibility. The gift of freedom that you and I enjoy was purchased with the sacrifices of our ancestors and contemporaries, upon battlefields too numerous here to describe in detail. The fight continues and will ever continue if freedom is to prevail.

"Those who contend that they have the right to disobey a law because it does not suit them or their group, those who trespass upon and destroy property, who by great numbers converge upon class rooms and campuses, take over and bring to a halt the great majority of students to study and try to get an education, these when measured by their conduct are found wanting in dignity and responsible citizenship.

"There has been a loud clamoring by those few that demand the right to lead us; yet they have never learned to follow—who demand the right to teach you, yet they have never been willing to learn. And they would teach and preach their doctrine of hate of America and all that she stands for—hate and contempt for her institutions, universities, governors, courts, and laws. They hammer away at our institutions even with torches of violence but these new leaders do not paint the rest of the picture. America with our states, counties, cities and schools have been used as a great anvil; the anvil outlasts the hammer.

"And so we come to begin this new year with more freedom, more privileges, and more liberty than any other people in the world. And if we are worth our salt, we will also accept the responsibility that goes with these blessings.

"One of the hard facts of life is that each generation must preserve its freedom or lose it. Democracy, by its very nature is based on the will of the people and history has proved that when a democracy fails, it generally does so because it has crumbled from within, rather than from without.

"There is no better purpose for us this day; there is no more noble decision that we can make than that we will dedicate ourselves anew, that we will be responsible citizens, that we will preserve these liberties and freedoms that we almost take for granted, that we will change and improve our government as changing conditions indicate such need, that we will shield her from those who would destroy this nation, that we who serve as trustees will pass them on unimpaired and unsoiled to our children and the generations of Americans yet unborn.

"I shall be content if, when my days are numbered, it can be truthfully said of me that with such ability as I possessed, I was faithful to that trust. And if we will all do that, then Democracy as we know it, the last fond hope of free people, will not perish from the face of the earth."

Chapter Eleven
Stories from the Bench

During all the social unrest that characterized the end of the sixties and early seventies, when it appeared as though society was splitting its seams, there was another kind of excitement taking place in the farming community of Jay, Florida, Santa Rosa County, just twenty miles from Milton. The noise coming from this locality was not the sound of demonstrators but the clanging and banging of drilling wells. Oil! Instead of haystacks sprouting out of a farmer's field there were pipes and pumps reaching down into the earth sucking out black, liquid gold which transferred into royalty checks for those fortunate enough to have leased their land.

Disputes over property and mineral rights ended up in court and often Woodrow had to settle it. One interesting situation arose over who owned the oil, gas, and mineral rights under a cemetery lot. The final decision came down in favor of the owner of the lot.

The first generation of wealth took their new found fortune in stride as they kept on farming while the money poured into the bank. Woodrow noted that the only change in their life-style was that they'd buy air-conditioned tractors with lights on them so they could plow at night and stay cool in the daytime.

One day the Mayor of Jay paid Woodrow a visit to ask his help. "Judge Melvin, you've known my mama a long time and you're the only one who might be able to change her mind."

"What's the problem?"

"For years now, since Daddy died, my brother and me have been chopping Mama's wood for that big ole wood stove in her kitchen. We're just plain tired of it, especially since the oil on the farm has made her a millionaire and she can afford a gas range and a gas heater. But she won't hear of it; too much money. Next time you're up in Jay would you mind stoppin' by and see if you can convince her to let loose of some of that money so we can get rid of that wood burning stove?"

Woodrow agreed and, in his soft spoken manner, approached the issue by asking his elderly friend, "Aren't you tired of worrying the boys about having to chop wood for this stove every day?"

"Never cooked on nothin' but a wood stove, Woodrow. My boys been choppin' wood since the day they could hold an axe."

"And I suspect they're getting' mighty tired of it; especially since these new gas ranges are so clean and convenient."

"And expensive! Land o' Mercy! Well over a hundred dollars."

"But think about it, you could visit the grandchildren, go into town, see some of your friends without worrying about keepin' the fire burning all day. I believe this oil money you receive every month could handle a new stove. I'd like to see you not to have to rely on those boys."

A moment of silence passed before the determined expression on this sweet mother's face turned to a hint of excitement. "It would be nice to get away for a day. And I am getting too old to bend over and sweep up the dirt they drag in from the woodpile. I'll just have to tighten my belt to pay for it."

Woodrow suppressed a smile and patted her hand. "Good choice; next time I visit you can brew me a cup of coffee on your new gas range."

Another instance involved an old woman who was a guardian of her mentally challenged brother. Like the mayor's mother, she was the recipient of all kinds of oil money but she petitioned the court to increase the allowance that she could spend on him. She came in with her lawyer. A.L. Johnson, and sat down and looked at Woodrow.

"You the judge here?"

"Yes, Ma'am

She turned to her lawyer and said, "A.L., you be quiet now; I know this boy's daddy was the tax assessor and I'll just talk to him."

Woodrow smiled at A.L. and turned to listen to the dear soul.

"I can't keep buying Willie pork chops the way they've gone up in price on the money I'm allowed. Lands sake he eats three, four at a time and he'd eat them three times a day if I could afford it. Have you priced a pair of overalls lately? And he kicks out shoes regularly. I could sure use an extra thirty-five dollars a month, Judge. Do you think that could be arranged?"

Woodrow assured her that she needed more than that and he'd see to it that the allowance was raised and she wouldn't have to keep coming back to town.

"I know it's really not convenient for you to come from Jay down to Milton so I'll fix it so you won't have to come back unless you want too. If you do, just call down here and my secretary will get you an appointment."

"Judge Melvin," she nodded her head toward A.L. "I told that lawyer I didn't need him."

***

A story that came out of the oil fields, told by Jim Barfield, a marshal of the District Court, relates the respect even the workers felt toward Woodrow.

"It all happened during the Jay oil boom when drilling crews rushed madly about. Our First District Court was holding court in Milton and on Wednesday afternoon the decision was made to ride over to Jay to see what was going on. Three judges and I got into a VW camper and headed north. We arrived at what looked like the largest rig being constructed when a worker dashed out and stopped us at the gate. I got out and explained that we were interested in seeing the operation. He immediately called over the 'big boss'.

"Hello, sir, I'm Jim Barfield, marshal of the District Court."

A huge muscular hand gripped mine as he looked at me out of the corner of one eye while keeping his attention on the rig with his other.

"As you can see, we're mighty busy here," he said.

"Yes, I can see that but I have three judges of the District Court of Appeal and we—"

"Big boss turned to his crew. '*Hey, Ben, put two more on the chain and move to the right a little*—Y'see marshal we just don't have time for visitors.'

"Yes, I see you're busy. We have Judge John Rawls here who is—"

"*Back the truck a little closer to the platform…*we're very busy right now and just don't have time to—"

"Yes, sir, and Judge Sam Spector is with us and he very much wanted to—"

"*Check the reading and see what it says*—I'm sorry; we're just too busy right now."

"Yes, sir, Judge Woodrow Melvin thought we might—"

Big Boss stopped shouting orders, looked me straight in the eye and said, "You mean you have Judge Melvin with you."

"I do."

With a booming voice, he issued a command. "*Hey you guys on the rig. Take a break for a few minutes. I'm bringing some visitors up.*'"

***

One of Woodrow's characteristics that set him apart was the attitude he demonstrated toward his work; no case was too big; no case was too small—regardless of the defendant. Each was tried justly in his courtroom. In 1975, his standard of ethics was put to the test in a high profile case involving a tax assessor in Okaloosa County. From the beginning it was an emotionally charged case and Woodrow found himself right in the middle of it.

Nita read the strained expression on her husband's face the minute he walked through the door on the evening of May 29,1975.

"Rhett Cadenhead is back in the country, Nita. It's all over the papers."

A gasp of surprise passed Nita's lips and she quizzed, "Did he come back on his own? How long has he been down there in Belize?"

"Eleven weeks."

"No doubt living high on the county's $35,000." Nita replied.

"According to The Okaloosa News Journal, he told the reporter he wanted to come back and straighten things out. He denied having left with vast sums of money. His attorney stated that Cadenhead returned voluntarily with the belief he is not guilty and he's willing to present his case to the citizens of Okaloosa County and specifically to those six citizens who will compose the jury in the trial."

"What would drive a man like Rhett to take off like that if he claims he's innocent of embezzlement?"

Woodrow removed his tie and loosened his shirt collar as he pondered the same question.

"Men do crazy things when the heats on, my dear. I expect it'll all come out at the trial. And by the way, I'm the only judge who agreed to take the case."

A look of exasperation on Nita's face preceded her response, "Woodrow Melvin, why am I not surprised?"

***

Two weeks later, the Okaloosa News Journal continued to report:

"Suspended Okaloosa County Tax Assessor, Rhett Cadenhead, standing before Judge Woodrow Melvin, entered a plea of no contest to two charges of

embezzlement Tuesday, June,17, with the stipulation that more than eighty other charges against him would be dropped.

Meeting for fifteen minutes in the judge's chambers with the Prosecutor James Russell, defense attorneys and Cadenhead, Melvin accepted the plea in open court.

The defendant agreed to repay all the money, approximately $38,000, the prosecution has alleged he embezzled over a four-and –a-half year period.

Cadenhead could receive a maximum of fifteen years on each of the two charges. "

A large majority of the public in Okaloosa County could not believe that their well-liked tax assessor, with all his political connections, could ever be convicted and they proceeded to bring pressure on the case by lobbying for him through letters and calls to newspapers throughout Florida. Because of Cadenhead's popularity, the state assigned James Russell, from St. Petersburg to handle the prosecution. He did his job; Cadenhead was found guilty. Now it was up to the judge to do his.

Nita fixed her husband his favorite meal the night before the sentencing. The smell of cornbread and frying fish brought Woodrow to the table but the fact that after several minutes of small talk he pushed a piece of mullet to the side of his plate and set down his utensils signaled concern.

"You're worried about sentencing Cadenhead tomorrow, aren't you, Woodrow?"

"It's weighed heavily on my mind all day, Nita, but I believe I've come to the only conclusion that's fair to the citizens of the county. You can't put people on the office payroll that didn't perform public service. His house maid was paid several thousand dollars; and that's only the tip of his iceberg. Now in his defense he agreed to pay back the money but it runs deeper than that. He has to understand that it doesn't matter how high you are in society you are accountable."

Nita shook her head in agreement. "Greed. Seems that once it gets hold of some folks it can lead to a heap of trouble."

"My secretary's been opening letters from his family and friends who think he ought not to go to prison but put him on probation. I don't think so. A public servant just can't steal money from the treasury and then be powder puffed on the wrist. What kind of an example would that set for other people. No, he's going to prison."

The atmosphere in the courtroom the following morning was electrifying. Not one seat was empty and standing room in the balcony was at its maximum. Extra security stood in strategic positions around the perimeter and the Florida media including the Associated Press sat poised and ready to record the days events.

As Judge Melvin entered the courtroom the bailiff commanded all to rise. An extraordinary amount of rustling and shuffling of feet echoed in Woodrow's ears and he caught his breath before asking all to be seated. A hush came over the crowd as eyes darted back and forth between Cadenhead and Woodrow.

Standing beside his lawyer, Rhett Cadenhead, who had pleaded guilty of embezzlement earlier, listened to Circuit Court Judge Woodrow Melvin pass sentence on him.

"Mr. Cadenhead, under the authority given to me by the state of Florida, I sentence you to serve ten years concurrently in the state prison. However, I will look favorably on a petition to reduce the sentence by half if you make full restitution to Okaloosa County."

A murmur ignited the pent-up tension felt by the observers in the courtroom and threatened to become louder and louder until Woodrow put a stop to it. As his gavel came down on the hard surface of his desk he declared, "I'll see you in my chambers, gentlemen."

Ray Helms, a Santa Rosa court clerk, who worked alongside Woodrow sensed that the atmosphere around the courthouse was not in the judge's favor and although some papers needed Judge Melvin's signature, he urged, "Judge, I'll come over here tomorrow and pick up those papers and take them back to Milton. Let's get out of here."

It was advice well heeded because when Helms did obtain

the paperwork he found it was done incorrectly. In all the commotion, had Woodrow signed it, there may have been a different outcome.

Chapter Twelve
Opposing Point of View

With all the accolades and honors Woodrow humbly accepted during his career such as Civilian of the Year, Man of the Year, the first recipient of the Chamber of Commerce Hall of Fame and even in a spirit of fun Aqua Rex 111, not everyone was full of gratitude for the influence he may have had in their lives; especially, if you were a defendant sentenced by Judge Melvin for a committed crime. On more than one occasion, Nita questioned her husband at the breakfast table.

"Woodrow, was I dreaming last night or did I hear the telephone ring around two-thirty?"

"Crank call, my dear. Nothing to worry your pretty little head about. Took me about a minute to go back to sleep."

"Somebody fussin' again?"

Woodrow took another sip of coffee, leaned toward his wife, patted her hand and said, "Nita, this is the only profession I know of where you can get along pleasing only half the people. Half win and the other half loses. And whenever they lose, they want to chew awhile. Blame somebody—they're not going to blame themselves."

Nita's shoulders shuddered, "I can't help but worry when these calls come in the middle of the night. Maybe it's time we used an unlisted number."

The muscles in Woodrow's brow tightened and his look became intense. "And give in to these scoundrels who hide in the dark ; I'll not let them intimidate our lives, Nita."

Woodrow pushed his chair back and rose from the table. "Gotta go; busy case load today."

Nita savored the kiss he placed on her cheek long after the screen door banged shut behind him. This was one morning ritual she wouldn't miss for anything.

As he drove into town, the breakfast conversation remained fresh in his mind. How could he tell Nita that just two days ago, an FBI officer stopped by his office to inform him that his life was in danger?

"Judge Melvin, as you know, drugs are not just a problem in south Florida but have infiltrated into northwest Florida as well."

"And I've dealt as heavily as the law allows with those who have been convicted."

"Yes, sir, and that's why I'm here."

Woodrow's questioning look urged the officer to continue. "The coast guard apprehended a ship off shore and your name as well as a prosecuting attorney over in Pensacola were on their hit list."

Woodrow raised his eyebrows and his attention quickened as he said, "Well, you don't say."

"Sir, this is serious business; these guys play for real. We urge you to be vigilant; report anything out of the ordinary. Do you own a gun?"

"Been deer hunting a time or two, but no, I don't possess a weapon."

The officer reached into a brief case, took out a pistol and placed it on the desk. "You do now. I recommend you get one of these deputies to take you out to the range for a little practice."

"That serious, huh?"

A slow smile spread across the officer's face as he once again stated the importance of his mission. "We need more judges like you who'll stand up to this scum—don't want to lose ya."

Not only seasoned drug dealers were displeased with Woodrow but one of the local gentry also had it in for him, too. A civil case tried in Woodrow's court had not turned out in this man's favor so he hired a hit man to bomb Judge Melvin. At the last moment he got cold feet and confessed.

"Judge, I couldn't do it. I swear I must have been drunk to agree in the first place. My conscience got a hold of me and I haven't slept for a week thinkin' 'bout it so this mornin' I made up my mind to come warn you. He's out to get ya."

Woodrow, in his calm manner, looked the fella over, asked him a few questions and decided the man was telling the truth. He picked up his phone and buzzed his secretary.

"Kathy, see if you can get the state attorney to come by my office; tell him it's a matter of importance."

Within an hour, the mole was wired to record conversation and instructed to act as though he intended to carry out the deed. A practice bombing out in the woods two days later blew the bark off a tree. That signaled the stake-out team to move in and arrest the guy for possessing a bomb.

When asked his reaction to the threat on his life, Woodrow replied, "It had to do with some civil case I'd tried; I never understood why he got hot under the collar about it. He felt he'd been done wrong, I guess. He was going to straighten me out or blow me up, one or the other. He'll have some time in prison to think about it."

The threats Woodrow received were delivered.

Simply going out to pick up the mail became a cause for concern. Three times the mailbox was blown to pieces and on one occasion the mailman almost became a victim. When Nita heard him shouting, "Judge Melvin, Judge Melvin," she came running from the kitchen out to the front steps, she stopped as her eyes focused on the mailman carrying a large pole with a rattlesnake curled around it.

"Land of Mercy! Where did you find that?"

"In your mailbox, ma'am. Almost bite me; scared me, too, but I carry an axe in my truck."

Nita's legs turned weak and she grabbed hold of the door.

"Woodrow, come out here!"

Shocked at the scene before him, Woodrow immediately understood the implication. "Can't thank you enough, Hank. More often than not, Nita goes out to pick up the mail. You okay, honey?"

Still shaken, she nodded, but added her own appreciation. "Throw that varmint over in the woods and come in and sit down. I'll get you some tea."

***

There were those defendants who thought that they could talk their way out of incarceration. Little did they realize that behind the soft spoken southern drawl and friendly looking face was a judge who possessed a keen sense of perception and was not easily fooled.

One fellow approached the bench for sentencing, carrying a Bible in his hands.

"Your Honor, may I speak?"

"You may."

Holding the Bible up in front of him he began, "As you can see, I read the Good Book every day now and it's made a new man of me. I'm changed; there's no need of me to go back to jail. I'm on the right track."

Woodrow looked at him with a compassionate smile on his face and said, "That's good, son, because where you're going, you're going to need the Lord."

Another citizen who had been picked for jury duty tried to pull the wool over Woodrow's eyes but soon found out that lying did not sit well with this judge. During the selection process he approached the bench and asked, "Judge Melvin, my wife is desperately sick. I don't need to be here; she needs me. The doctor has written her a prescription and I need to pick it up and take it straight to her."

Judge Melvin told him he was excused. It was nine o'clock in the morning. When it came time for lunch, Woodrow walked into the Café, looked for an empty table and spotted the excused juror sitting with the sheriff.

Keeping his eyes on the man, Woodrow walked over and asked, "Have you been home yet?"

Guilt washed over his reddening face as he answered, "No, sir, but I'm fixin' to go."

Woodrow looked at him and delivered the punch. "Before you go, come by the office because you're in contempt of court."

However, of all the cases that went through his court, the ones that anguished him the most were the custody cases. With five children of his own, he had a heart for children and many nights he woke up wondering if he was sending the youngsters in the right direction.

Awakened by his tossing and turning, Nita understood the reason and softly asked, "Woodrow, do you want to talk? Some custody case is weighing heavily on your mind isn't it?"

"I'm sorry to waken you, sweetheart, but you're right. You know if two grown people don't want to live together I'm not too worried about that; but these little kids get caught up in the web of circumstances. Whatever happens between the husband and the wife in so far as it relates to the children is important. I'm not sure in this case if either parent is qualified; might have to figure out which set of grandparents will do the best job."

"Is the child old enough for you to talk to and get a feel for the situation from his perspective?"

"Yes, he's old enough to understand there's major friction going on because of him." Woodrow closed his eyes and sighed, "Lord, forgive the guilt we lay on our children's young shoulders. In their innocence, they suffer; sometimes for a lifetime. Please help me make the right decision."

***

Woodrow came out of his office, his eyes watery and a warm glow to his face; as he handed his secretary a piece of paper, he said, "Read this Kathy. They're few and far between in my line of work so since you're my right arm, I want you to share in it, too."

Kathy read it through and her eyes filled with tears. "You need to frame that one, Judge Melvin."

Woodrow nodded. "Very few times does anybody ever come back and say 'thank you.' Doesn't happen. This fellow expected to go to prison and I put him on probation; it was a marginal case. Maybe I hesitated before I finally decided to put him on probation and he could see that it was nip and tuck. Good to hear that he has a job and is married with a family. He just wanted to say thanks, I guess. That gives me great satisfaction."

Kathy smiled at the judge as he turned to retreat to his office. "A job well done, sir."

"All in a day's work, Kathy." His door shut behind him.

Chapter Thirteen
A 'Judge's Judge'

An old adage states that "Cream rises to the top"; and Woodrow's fellow judges showed their admiration and respect for their fellow peer by electing him to serve, at different stages of his career, on the Board of Governors of the Florida Bar, as Chairman of the Florida Conference of Circuit Judges and as Chief Circuit Judge of the First District. Known among his colleagues as 'a judge's judge', the highest honor entrusted to him was Chairman of the Florida Judicial Qualifications Committee.

His work with the commission involved investigating complaints made against judges. If the charges were found valid; then the accused judge appeared before the commission hearing, and, if found guilty, would be recommended for discipline by the Supreme Court of Florida.

Woodrow explained, "The work of the commission is comparable to that of a grand jury. Grand juries investigate many cases that never see the light of day because there is nothing to them. Many of the complaints the commission investigates are not valid; they come from people unsatisfied with a judge's ruling.

"I've seen, in my time as chairman, a judge resign rather

than go to a hearing. He'd break under the strain of his office and not have control of his mental faculties; without intending to, he'd be mistreating people. We'd get him off the bench real fast unless he agreed to treatment. If he would seek help, the state paid for it. We saved several judges who were just under stress— too much work, not enough time or help to do it. In those regards, the commission has really served a great purpose in Florida. It's been a safety valve; but then it's also been a protection for judges from unjust criticism."

In the 'law community', Judge Melvin set the standard for other circuit court judges. Allen Lindsay, a Milton attorney, recalled an event that substantiated this fact.

"In the early seventies I was in Melbourne, Florida, at the grand opening of the Holiday Inn on I-95. I was introduced to then Chief Justice Vassar Carlton, who, when he found out I was from Milton, asked me about Woodrow Melvin. He said, *"Judge Melvin is the best judge in Florida; I didn't say the best Circuit Judge in Florida, I said the best judge in Florida."*

"Those are high marks from a man who held the most prestigious position in the Florida judicial system."

What was the measuring stick Woodrow used to quantify not only his performance but other judges as well? A speech he gave at an investiture ceremony reveals the attitude that penetrated his work.

"Judge Anderson, on behalf of my brother judges, I welcome you to the circuit bench of Florida. Shortly after I became a judge, I read an article authored by the Honorable Edward J. Devitt, Chief Judge of the United States District for the District of Minnesota. It is written for a similar occasion, and what I'm about to say is an abbreviated and slightly modified version of his Commandments for a new judge.

First Commandment
Be Kind

If we judges could possess but one attribute, it should be a kind and understanding heart. The bench is no place for a cruel or callous man regardless of his other qualities and abilities.

Second Commandment
Be Patient

Patience is one of the cardinal virtues, and it should be one of the most important commandments for the judge. We must constantly keep in mind the marked displeasure we felt as practicing lawyers for the judges who wouldn't hear us out. We owe it to the lawyer to let him make his point. Minding our own business and permitting the lawyer to mind his is an essential corollary of patience.

Third Commandment
Be Dignified

You must possess an appreciation of the great prestige of the judicial office and of the respect which it is accorded. People generally, and lawyers as well, want to look up to their judges. They want to admire and respect him for his ability as a judge and for the way he runs his court. So long as he knows the public's regard for the judicial office, the conscientious judge will conduct himself fittingly.

Fourth Commandment
Don't take yourself too seriously

The transition from bar to bench is a big one and making the change with equilibrium is not always the easiest task. We must keep our heads about us. Federal Circuit Court Judge Harold R. Medina once commented:

"After all is said and done, we cannot dent the fact that a judge is almost of necessity surrounded by people who keep telling him what a wonderful fellow he is. And if he once begins to believe it, he is a lost soul."

Fifth Commandment
Remember that a lazy judge is a poor judge

The road to success on the bench is the same as in any field of human endeavor. It must be characterized by hard work. Some people, and many lawyers, think that a judgeship is a form of retirement for the hard-working practitioner. That, of course, is not the case.

Sixth Commandment
Don't be dismayed when reversed

One of the most shocking experiences which awaits the trial judge is opening the morning mail to find a slip opinion of the Appellate Court in one of his cases, at the bottom of which he sees the ominous word 'Reversed'. When it happens to you a few times, you might come to the honest realization that in some instances the appellate court is justified in reversing you. Every so often, even these august appellate judges make mistakes and substitute their findings for those of the trial court. The law says they can't do this; but they do! You should view their folly with tolerance.

Here is a word of advice about reversals, Don't keep track of them. Such record-keeping may make you too cautious—so sensitive to committing error that it deprives you of the intellectual courage which should be the hallmark of a good trial judge.

Seventh Commandment
Remember there are no unimportant cases

This is another way of saying that you must give the same conscientious attention to every matter that comes before you. We may think cases can be classed as important and unimportant, but the litigants do not feel that way. Their case is very important to them and it must be to us.

Eighth Commandment
Neither cause nor condone unnecessary delay
It is our responsibility to maintain current dockets so that equal justice for all will be insured by prompt justice to all.

Ninth Commandment
Pray for Divine guidance
If you believe in a supreme being, you should pray to him for guidance. Judges need all the help they can get.

In later years, Woodrow was asked by a reporter what he would say if he had to write a job description for a judge. He made these remarks:

"A judge would have to be well versed in the jurisdiction of the court and the matters that would come before that court. The main thing I would say to a young judge comin' aboard would be to keep his feet on the ground and to bear in mind that everybody that comes in there is human and they're entitled to be treated fairly. And don't pay any attention to all the accolades that just naturally come your way as a judge because they don't mean anything. They keep telling you what a good judge you are and what good decisions you're making and how important you are; if you pay any attention to that stuff, you're lost. The best thing any judge can do, particularly any young judge, is to remember to keep a clear mind and stay humble because you have a lot of discretionary power. It's awesome. It's almost irreversible discretionary power that a judge has and if you couple that with a big head, you've got problems. So I guess that would be some do's and don'ts—not necessarily a job description because a job description sets out what you are to do. What's important is your attitude."

***

There was one young lady, close to Woodrow's heart, that he especially wanted to see start out on the right track.

"Laura," Woodrow put down the book he was reading as the door opened and he welcomed his eldest daughter into his office. "What's on your mind?"

"I made a life-changing decision while I was in Shalimar today. I was sent over to do the court recording and as I listened to the lawyers present their cases, I realized I can do that. I want to apply to law school, Dad. What do you think? Do I have what it takes?"

Laura had her father's rapt attention. "Laura, you've always been able to do whatever you put your mind too. Have you thought this thing through? You have a six-year-old son in first grade."

"Yes, I have weighed the pros and cons and I believe I can do it."

"Your mother and I will support you whatever the need. But I want you to remember, there may be a crowd, but there's always room at the top. I, however, cannot take the first test for you; can't try the first case or present the first argument."

Laura nodded her head in agreement. "I want to do this on my own merit, Dad. Mac did it on his."

Woodrow's lips turned into a teasing smile. "Look out, Mac. Your sister is hot on your heels."

Laughter had the final word as Laura gave her father an affectionate hug.

Ten years later, in the judge's chamber, Woodrow and Laura once again shared a special father/daughter bond.

"Just one more picture, sir," the photographer looked through the lens of his camera. "We're making history; 1990 is the year Florida's 1st Circuit Court has its first father/daughter team."

Nita, proud of her daughter, could not contain her enthusiasm. "And don't forget she's only the second woman circuit court judge in the First Circuit."

Woodrow looked at his watch and then turned to Laura and with a sparkle in his eyes said, "Time to go into the court room, honey. It's not every day a father gets to administer the judge's oath to his daughter."

Judge Woodrow Melvin
and his daughter Judge Laura Melvin

***

Not every moment in a court room is solemn and serious. Humor can be as unexpected as a sudden rain shower and just as refreshing. Nita, always anxious to hear how a case went, relished the time spent with Woodrow, especially after he returned from presiding over an out-of-town case. She often greeted him at the door, "Well, how was Miami, Woodrow?"

"Busy; seems every time I go down there, the traffic gets worse. Glad we live in Santa Rosa County and not Dade."

"Refresh my memory but what was the case about, again?"

Woodrow put down the newspaper and explained, "A man almost got killed at a railroad crossing so he sued the railroad. You'll never guess who the lawyer was that represented him."

Nita's face went blank as she shook her head. "No idea."

"Robert Floyd."

A gasp came from Nita and she continued, "But he's a judge, isn't he. You know him well."

"Tells me puttin' three kids through college on a judge's salary wasn't enough so he went back into private practice. Wish you could've been there, Nita; the funniest thing happened."

Woodrow started chuckling and Nita anxious to hear the story, urged him on.

"Tell me. Tell me."

"It seems there was a defect in the electrical system and the bells were not ringing and the lights were not flashing on this signal in Polk County. Now this is phosphate country and you know phosphate is a powdery gray and covers everything. The evidence was that it was also a foggy day. So you had foggy weather and a gray gondola parked across the road with no flashing lights. This fella came along in an eighteen wheeler, plowed into it and near about killed the hell out of him.

"The lawyers representing the railroad made an objection and I was a little slow rulin' and Floyd, my friend from the circuit court, was associate counselor representin' the plaintiff. His co-counselor said, "Your Honor, I object to that." Floyd jumped up, hit the table and yelled, "Sustained!"

"It wasn't any of his business but he had just been on the bench so long that he sustained his own partners objections." Woodrow laughed aloud. "You know I never had that happen before but it sure was hard to keep a straight face."

Chapter Fourteen
On to a Higher Court

At one time, the Florida judicial system was made up of a hodge-podge of different types of court. Justice of the Peace, Municipal, Special, and Constitutional Court of Record are a few of the many that encumbered the swift operation of justice. The system needed to be streamlined.

This issue first came to Woodrow's attention when he was working in the legislature and he was selected to assist in writing amendments to Article V, the division of the Constitution dealing with judicial matters. Out of this assignment came a unified system which introduced the courts of appeal. Up to this point, cases on appeal from the circuit court went directly to the Supreme Court which became over-loaded and cumbersome. To solve the problem, an intermediate appellate court was introduced.

In 1977, Governor Reubin Askew, appointed Woodrow to take an active role in the very legislative process he helped establish. He filled a new appellate judgeship created by the legislature because of the increasing number of cases coming before the court from thirty-seven North Florida counties stretching from Jacksonville to Pensacola.

When asked by the Summation, a newspaper of the

Escambia-Santa Rosa Bar Association, how he felt about moving up to the First District Court, he responded: "I'm leaving my beloved hometown and local judgeship with mixed emotions, but I look forward to the new experience of serving the people of Northwest Florida in a wider area and greater capacity."

Always sensitive to Nita's feelings about career changes, Woodrow watched as she took a photo of their children down from the wall and placed it in her suitcase.

"You're going to miss them, aren't you?" he asked.

"Of course. But it's not as though they're dependent on us now; they've all made their career choices and have gone their own way. We'll always be family, no matter where we are. Besides, I wouldn't want you to miss this challenge for all the tea in China. Woodrow, do you realize by becoming an appellate court judge you've made your law circle complete. How many lawyers can make that claim?

When Woodrow looked at his wife, his endearing smile told her how grateful he was for a partner who understood his personality and willingly supported his ventures.

"It'll be a little like old times, won't it dear?" she responded. "I wonder if anyone will remember us?"

Nita need not have worried; Tallahassee put out the welcome mat. Absence from the state capital had not diminished the esteem and respect the citizens felt toward Woodrow. His reputation was intact as evidenced by an article in the Tallahassee Democrat, August 24, 1977.

Deserving Promotion

We applaud Governor Askew's promotion of Circuit Court Judge Woodrow Melvin Sr. to the First District Court of Appeals which serves all North Florida.

We in Tallahassee remember Judge Melvin as a diligent and skillful assistant attorney general in the 1940's, an effective member of the House and Senate during the 1950's, and have taken note of his service as a respected judge in a circuit court to our west these past 21 years. He was chairman of the State Judicial Qualifications Commission which in recent years has been the key element in policing the ethical conduct of Florida judges.

His record placed him at the top of the list of three names submitted by the Judicial Nominating Commission for the additional First District judgeship created by the 1977 Legislature.

We are glad the Governor chose him because, though he is approaching normal retirement age at 64, he will bring a fine judicial temperament and a maturity of judgment to our appellate bench to cap a distinguished career.

On September 2, 1977, at 11:00 o'clock a.m. in the court room of the First District Court of Appeal, Judge Woodrow Melvin stood before family, friends and peers to be invested as the seventh jurist on the appellate court. His response echoed the familiar theme that he so staunchly believed in all his life.

"If it may please the court, Your Excellency, Governor Askew, Mr. Chief Justice Overton, Chief Judge McCord, and Your Honors, distinguished members of the legislature, executive and branches of our government, fellow attorneys, distinguished guests, ladies and gentlemen, "I would like to take this opportunity to express my keen appreciation to the nominating commission of the First District Court of Appeal for having included my name among those listed for the Governor's consideration. Thank you, Governor Askew for the confidence and trust you evidenced by appointing me to serve as a member of this court. To serve in this judiciary, to me, is the highest honor that could come my way. Our judicial system, imperfect certainly, is the greatest assurance of the continuation of government based upon law rather than the changing whims or fancies of any man.

"When man first wronged another, that set in motion an endless search to find a more perfect system of government. There is ingrained in every human soul a desire for justice. Man can endure hardships untold and pain and suffering beyond imagination, as through the ages countless millions have done. But he has never willingly tolerated a situation where wrong takes the place of that which is right. We find the Egyptian Code of Meaneys, a translation of which still exists and is recognized as the world's oldesst code. Then history points to the Mosaic Code, the Babylonian code of Hammurabi, the ancient codes of the Chinese and Greeks, the Justinian Code of Rome, the Napoleonic Code, the Magna Carta, the Common Law of England, the Mayflower Compact, our own Declaration of Independence, the Constitution of the United States, the constitutions and laws of our fifty states. All of these are milestones along the road traveled in mankind's unquenchable thirst for justice and liberty under law. Justice and freedom 'under law' is America's answer to that voice.

"So, we are privileged to have a government based on law, consisting of three branches: the Legislative Law Writing Branch, chosen by the people for that purpose, the Executive Law Enforcing and Administrative Branch, chosen by the people for that purpose, and the Judicial Branch, chosen by the people to sit in judgment as to their rights and responsibilities based upon the Constitution and related laws. The members of each branch have taken the same oath of office to support, protect and defend the constitution and laws of the United States and of the state of Florida. No one may in reason expect a judge to stray from the court's constitutional jurisdiction, and write with a legislative pen. With each branch working in its constitutionally assigned field of labor, realizing that neither should or could shackle or dilute the other. Government under law, as we have been privileged to know it, will be passed unimpaired to the hands of those who are preparing, I hope, to receive it.

"With each branch working in harmony toward that common goal, we might give heed to what the prophet Micah wrote. Perhaps he summarized the whole subject in a few words when he said, "What doth the Lord thy God require but that you do justice, that you love mercy, and that you walk humbly before thy God."

***

The scenario in the appellate court was different—no bailiff, no court reporters, no jury, no plaintiff, no defendants – only judges and one or more lawyers. Thirty-seven counties generated 2,000 appeals annually. Each of the seven appellate judges were responsible for rendering a decision on 350 cases and since individual cases are heard as a triumvirate, each judge had to be familiar with 700 other cases as well. It was a highly responsible position but it had a low profile. In 1978, an election year, that was a problem for Woodrow. His term of office was about to expire and due to a change in the method of electing judges, he found his biggest opponent was himself. It was almost the biggest upset in all the years his name had appeared on a ballot and it garnered much press coverage. The Tallahassee Democrat, November 5, 1978, explained the circumstances.

Judge Melvin Faces Unusual Election

When it came to elections, Woodrow Melvin had it pretty easy during his twenty-one years as a circuit court judge in the Florida Panhandle. He was elected in 1952 without any opposition and then he was re-elected three times without having to face an opponent. Now things are different.

Melvin is a district court of appeal judge in Tallahassee. His term is just about up. And because of a constitutional amendment passed in 1976, Melvin is pitted against the first opponent he has faced in 21 years. He gets to run against himself.

The unusual election is the result of a merit retention system for appellate judges. Tuesday's ballot simply will ask voters whether Melvin should be retained as an appellate judge. Below that question will be two answers: 'For retention' and Against retention.' If a majority votes 'for', then Melvin stays on the bench

111

for another six years. If a majority votes 'against', then Melvin leaves and a replacement will be appointed by the governor.

So the question in this race isn't who to vote for. It is whether a 65 year-old judge who grew up in the Panhandle, served in the State House and Senate, has been a judge for more than 20 years, and is nearing retirement age should stay on the job.

When asked for his comment, Melvin said, "I guess the whole theory of the matter is you're running on your own merits. I'm willing to lay whatever my reputation may be on the line. An appellate judge's record often is not closely watched by the public. Cases on appeal deal only with possible trial or administrative errors. The appellate judge's ruling deals solely with the law instead of the more dramatic actions that can go on in a courtroom and bring attention to a trial judge.

An appellate judge's record can also be difficult to gauge because lawyers are understandably hesitant to speak out against a judge they may have to argue a case before."

Quotations from several newspapers revealed the support they willingly gave Woodrow and strongly urged the public to keep Judge Melvin on the bench.

The Tallahassee Democrat, November 5, 1978

The Santa Rosa Free Press, Nov.2, 1978 wrote:

Judge Melvin is a well-respected, fair, honest, dedicated jurist. We remember him not only for his judicial leadership but as a professional friend. He never severed his ties with his friends and neighbors, although he never let them influence his search for the truth or the dispensation of justice wherever it may have been. Besides, we like him because he's a home-town boy.

However, we are also influenced by what other

professionals have to say. Among members of the Florida Bar, a query resulted in a 92 percent recommendation from those attorneys who have had occasion to serve before him . We are impressed; we present him for your approval.

The Santa Rosa Free Press, Nov.2, 1978

The Tallahassee Democrat, November 4, 1978 reported an interview with Woodrow:

When interviewed, Woodrow Melvin replied, *"In judicial elections, Florida Bar canons of ethics severely limit what a candidate can and can't say. Still, incumbents get off the bench and go out of the courtroom long enough for voters to look them over and try to attach a little personality to their judicial postures. Merit retention changes all that.*

There's no way to run a race; there really aren't any issues except qualifications. You can't promise how you're going to rule. So I'm staying in here doing what I've been doing—keeping up with my job. That's about all I can do.

Being 65 doesn't have anything to do with it. It's being willing to work. I am current with my reading. I study all the time. I know the day will come when my productive days are numbered, but as long as I'm healthy, I want to work. I want to wear out; I don't want to rust out."

The Tallahassee Democrat, November 4, 1978.

When the election was over, the victory was his, but the margin was slim. The final tally showed 184,000 votes for retention and 154,000 against. The question of the day was 'why?' Woodrow had never come this close to losing in all these years of public service.

William C. Mansfield, editorial page editor of the Tallahassee Democrat, offered a logical explanation:

113

"One small figure—10,785 tells the story of Tuesday's constitutional amendment balloting in Florida. That figure represents the number of people in Leon County who voted to oust Woodrow Melvin from the First District Court of Appeal. It also represents 38 percent of the vote on that question.

"Did that many local voters really disapprove of Judge Melvin's conduct on the bench? It's extremely difficult to believe they did. During the entire campaign we heard or read not a single word of criticism about Judge Melvin. We did hear words of praise for him and read of the high rating he got from members of the Florida Bar who actually practice in his court.

"It's much more likely that Judge Melvin, like a number of worthy constitutional amendments, was a victim of voter confusion. The levers under the judge's name were labeled exactly the same as those under the amendments: 'for' and 'against'. Many voters apparently slapped down all the 'against' levers to be sure they defeated specific amendments they either opposed or did not understand.

"Judge Melvin was fortunate; he got more 'for' than 'against' votes. No constitutional amendment was that fortunate."

Chapter Fifteen
Judicial Opinions

One significant difference between a courtroom judge and an appellate court judge is, if an appeal is made, the judge on the appellate court must write an opinion or review of what a trial court had decided.

The trial hears the witnesses, looks at the evidence, hears the argument of law and a decision is made by either the jury or the judge. If a party does not agree, they take it to the appellate court. This court will review the record; but they don't hear any evidence, they don't hear witnesses, they don't empanel a jury. It is just cold transcript of everything that happened in the trial court. Three judges go over this information; and then they may hear argument from the attorneys once a brief has been presented. Each case will then be assigned to a primary judge; and he will write an opinion; it is his view of the facts and the law. His decision could be affirmed, in other words, agree with what the trial court did and leave it alone, or reverse it with directions to the court about what they did wrong. After the opinion has been written, he circulates it to the next judge who looks at it; and if he agrees will sign off on it. If he doesn't agree, he writes his own opinion and now there are two. Those two go to the third judge who agrees with one of the two appellate jurists. Now there are two concurring and one dissenting jurist but the result of the majority is that the decision of the appellate court is 2 to 1."

Even before Woodrow was officially assigned to the appellate court, there were occasions when he was asked to fill in for a jurist. In 1971, he was asked to be the primary judge in the following appeal and it demonstrated once again his sense of fairness and his determination to maintain the rights of the individual.

Excerpts from the opinion printed in Volume 248 Southern Reporter, page 515 present the situation as Judge Melvin wrote it:

On December 24, 1969, the Appellant, Roosevelt Stride Jacobs, hereafter referred to as the Defendant, was arrested by a member of the police department of Jacksonville as a suspect in connection with a pending investigation of a homicide and was placed in jail. After being detained in jail for six days, the Defendant was asked by a sergeant if he didn't feel like he needed an attorney. The inquiry of the officer and his new-found concern for the Defendant's welfare came a bit late. The record reveals that from the time Defendant, who has a fourth grade education, was placed in jail, until the time he finally had the benefit of the advice of his attorney, the officers obtained three separate statements from him. The Defendant was not carried before a magistrate until after his indictment on January 9, 1970. The State successfully offered the three statements in evidence at Defendant's trial, over the objections of his counsel. The remainder of the State's case was constructed upon circumstantial evidence.

Woodrow drew upon the opinion concerning a similar situation in Dawson v. State, Volume 139 Southern Reporter, p. 408 to clarify his decision.

"The right of a free man to be presented to a sworn judicial officer promptly upon his arrest is not a technical or trivial right. Such rights are the bedrock of our liberties and have grown out of mankind's experiences over hundreds of years.

These rights are so fundamental in our concept of justice that they are embodied in the written laws of every state in this nation. I cannot accept the proposition that the lawmakers, in enacting statues, such as these, ever intended that the positive mandate of immediate presentment could be ignored by the public officials if the evidence showed the ultimate product to be otherwise voluntary. Practical men know that the question of whether a confession is freely and voluntarily made is determined by weighing the evidence produced by those who obtained the confession and are responsible for it. Every person who can read is familiar with the methods used in some area of the world to obtain confessions. The methods there used have become commonly known as brainwashing. We have not applied that definition in this country but the evidence revealed by the record in this case makes it rather difficult to distinguish what has happened here from what often happens there. The mandates of the written law are as clear as the noon day sun and it certainly is imposing no hardship upon the sworn officers of the law to require their adherence to it. Moreover, prompt adherence to the requirements of the law in every instance would add immensely to the validity of a confession thereafter obtained and would remove from the minds of judge and jury many of the doubts and uncertainties so often present in these cases."

Woodrow gave additional insight into the case.

"The Defendant was tried upon the indictment charging him with murder in the first degree. The jury returned its verdict finding the Defendant guilty of murder in the second degree."
"The ground is level before the Bar of Justice. In dealing with its citizens, the State of Florida must conduct itself with the same degree of rectitude as is required by the State of its citizens. The State may take no pride in a judgment of conviction that is the product of uneven justice.
"The officers investigating this case persisted in defiance of the clear mandate of the Legislature of Florida and refused to hear the clear warning sounded by the courts of this state. The

117

result was the obtaining of three statements from the Defendant.

"The law is certain. The duty of this court is clear. We now hold that the alleged statements referred to above are not competent evidence and that the presentation thereof to the jury shattered beyond repair this Defendant's basic right to a fair and impartial trial. The judgment and sentence appealed from is reversed, and a new trial is granted the Defendant.

Woodrow's ability and willingness to take very difficult stands when he saw the law was clear did not go unnoticed and Judge John T. Wigginton agreed with Woodrow and sent him a letter affirming his decision.

"Dear Woodrow,
Re: Roosevelt Strike Jacobs v. State- N-289

I have just reviewed and concurred in the excellent opinion which you wrote in connection with the above appeal. If permitted to stand against assault in the Supreme Court on certiorari, it will be recognized as a landmark decision in Florida. I want to commend you for the excellent quality of its composition and the clear expression of the law as we have held it to be.

Let me again thank you for the prompt manner in which you have dispatched the cases assigned to you. Our court is grateful for your help.

Sincerely,
John T. Wigginton

***

There were many instances when an appeal was affirmed by Judge Melvin and the decision of the trial court was not changed. Excerpts from the following opinion, written by Woodrow with his subtle sense of humor, run parallel to the discussion of the charges.

"The record reveals that Officer Jefferson entered the men's restroom at the Jacksonville Greyhound Bus Station for the purpose of checking with reference to drug activity and other unlawful behavior. The officer testified that the defendant was inside a locked pay toilet stall. The officer testified that the defendant's feet were pointing in a direction that was completely inconsistent with the location of a person's feet using any of the facilities in the pay toilet. The officer then looked through a half-inch crack that existed between the door and the wall of the toilet stall and saw the defendant holding a belt around his arm so that his veins would become extended. The officer further noted that the defendant was introducing into his veins some type of injection. Thereupon the officer, with the assistance of the manager of the station, unlocked the stall and placed the defendant under arrest. Inside the stall were found a cap cooker and a match box lying on the toilet paper container. These articles contained cocaine and were seized. The only question presented here for review is whether the surveillance by the officer and seizure of the articles under the circumstances stated, constituted an unreasonable surveillance and search.

The officer had a legal right to be in the public bathroom and to observe anything that was in his plain view. The record reveals the officer's testimony.

Q. When you stopped outside the toilet, how big a crack was there? (Crack between the toilet stall and the door.)
A. I'd say half an inch."
Q. You were able to stand outside the stall and look through that crack, and in plain view, you saw him with the needle in his arm and his belt around his arm. Is that correct?"
A. Yes, sir."
Q. How far away from the crack were you? Did you have to get close to it?"
A. No, I didn't have to peep. There's about a three-foot aisle in between the wash basin and toilets, so by me walking down the middle of the aisle, it puts me about

119

six or eight inches in front of the stall."

Q So you are about six to eight inches away?"

A. All I had to do was look as I walked by."

"The Constitution of Florida grants to all persons the right to be secure against unreasonable searches and seizures. When an officer is in place where he has the lawful right to be and he observes within plain view a person engaged in the commission of a felony, or engaged in an activity which causes the officer reasonably to believe that a felony is then being committed, the officer has a right then and there to arrest such person. The defendant urges, however, that the act of the officer in looking through the crack in the door constituted an unlawful search. It did not.

"The officer did not owe the defendant any duty to announce that his activity was about to be observed. The defendant chose the toilet stall as a place where he would administer the shot of cocaine. His vision was not as keen or attentive as that of the officer. He selected a stall that had a one-half inch crack in the door through which one could easily observe his activity.

"*The defendant made a poor choice. He pointed his life and his feet in the wrong direction.* (Emphasis supplied)

"The method of surveillance by the officer in this case was legal. The trial court therefore correctly ruled in denying the defendant's motion to suppress. Therefore, the judgment and sentence appealed from are affirmed."

***

One evening, while sitting with Nita, Woodrow blinked his eyes, rubbed them until they watered, then set the newspaper he'd been reading down beside him. His actions caught his wife's attention and she looked at him. Concern wrinkled her brow as she inquired, "Woodrow, is something wrong? Are you not feeling well? You usually read the paper from cover to cover."

"My eyes are itching and burning. I'm having trouble concentrating on the print. It feels a little troublesome. Call Mac and see if you can't get me an appointment to have them checked the next time we're in Milton, will you, dear? Helps to have an ophthalmologist in the family, I reckon."

The news Dr. Melvin gave his brother confirmed what Woodrow had suspected for some time; eye strain and age had taken their toll.

"I'm not surprised, Mac. After two years of reading pages and pages of transcripts, the strain's been too much. It's a whole lot easier to sit there for five days and listen, as trial judges do, than to read five days of court testimony. I suppose I'm faced with the issue of retirement."

Mac placed his arm around his elder brother's shoulder and gave him a hug. "No disgrace big brother; we all have to face it sooner or later."

"You know, Mac I never had any desire to hold a permanent job on the state Supreme Court. I got as high as I wanted to go, and that's not with any disrespect to the Supreme Court. This is what I wanted to wind up my career doing. It's the highest honor to come my way and I'm deeply grateful."

A month later, while attending a reunion day ceremony for former senators, Woodrow collapsed and was rushed to the hospital and suffered an angina attack. But it wasn't just the physical symptoms of an aging body that urged Woodrow to leave Tallahassee. He missed Santa Rosa County, his friends, and most of all his home by the sparkling blue, mullet-filled waters of Blackwater Bay. He joked as he left the capital, "I've got a cast net in my car. Fishing is my hobby; mullet fishing is what I really like."

Retirement:
At home on his beloved Blackwater Bay.

***

Ironically, the net seldom got wet. He was back in Milton a total of two weeks before he was asked to return to the bench to help other judges in Santa Rosa County with their heavy caseloads by doing recall work. The circuit court missed Woodrow and the feeling was mutual. Before long he was working almost full-time again.

"Woodrow", Nita sighed, "You're not foolin' me. All that talk about wantin' to cast a net—mullet-fishing being your hobby. There's only one hobby on your mind twenty-four hours a day and that's law. Always has been and always will be.

"You may be right, my dear; all I know is that rockin' chair sittin' over yonder doesn't fit me."

"Promise me one thing, Woodrow?"

"Don't take every case that comes down the pike."

A reassuring smile from her husband calmed her anxiety. "I

122

paid my dues, sweetheart; no worry there."

At 78 years of age, a new avenue of service surfaced in Woodrow's career. He was full of enthusiasm as he received his certification in mediation and had an answer for any critic who wondered why he needed to help people make their own decisions after all the years he'd spent making decisions for them.

With a familiar chuckle and sparkle in his blue eyes he responded, "Colonel Sanders was 65 when he decided to start selling chickens."

All the "retirement" activity did not come without a price. Not only did Woodrow contend with the angina problem but he triumphed over gall bladder cancer, two knee replacements, skin cancer and for the last seven years of his life he dealt with the complications of sugar diabetes. For the average person his age, these health problems would have been enough to call it a day. For Woodrow, they were simply bumps in the road and he would find either a way through them or around them.

As he explained, "It's always been our philosophy that we're going to live with something rather than die from it. You can't do anything about it so there's no sense getting' down and out about it. When I had cancer in the gall bladder I asked the doctor, because I wasn't too inclined to get involved in all that radiation ordeal, if I could sit it out. What were my odds?" He says, 'Well, you can take this course in radiation here twice a day for six weeks. I'll think you'll be alright; if you don't, I think it'll take your life in about two years'. I said, 'Hey, I can understand that. When do I start?'"

***

A spirit of finality hung in the air on a cool, December morning in 1993 as Woodrow, almost reverently, carried his official letter of resignation addressed to the Chief Justice, to the mailbox. In his humble, unpretentious manner, Woodrow quietly left the bench after thirty-six years. Finally, time was his own;

time to spend with his beloved Nita, time to attend the weekly Kiwanis club lunches where he kept in touch with friends and time to sit and enjoy the natural ebb and flow of life around Blackwater Bay. For a man who'd been a "workaholic" all his life, the adjustment was not easy. The inner servant part of his nature struggled with this new-found freedom as Woodrow explained, "I have too much time on my hands now. My mind is still active and I feel I should be doing something for somebody, but I'm not."

When asked if he would take the same career path, Woodrow was eager to say, "Yes. I think Nita and I made a difference in our work; it's been very satisfying. I believe I did a good job. Every case meant something to somebody and every case was important. And if it was decided correctly for that person, those were the highlights of my career."

Long before Woodrow ever sat on the bench, just as he was preparing to leave for law school, a gentleman knowing the financial struggle Woodrow faced, gave him an overcoat to keep him warm. When Woodrow asked how he could repay him, the man replied, "Just pass it along." Woodrow never stopped passing it. He wore the material in that coat bare but the attitude of caring and compassion it represented was the fabric of his life.

Florida Supreme Court Justice Parker Lee McDonald in the September issue of the Summation described Judge Melvin best when he wrote, "A person who is warm, cordial, witty, compassionate, understanding, intelligent, fair and considerate is liked by nearly everyone. Thus, I like and respect Woodrow Melvin. I have seen Woodrow lead the legislature, the conference of circuit judges, and preside as a judge. I know of the great contributions he has made as a judge judging the conduct of other judges. I know of the devotion he has shown to his wife and the pride he has in his family. When I think of Woodrow Melvin, I am warmed and feel good. I admire him and treasure him as a friend. If ever a judge earned the title "Honorable", Woodrow Melvin certainly has."

Parker Lee McDonald, Justice Florida Supreme Court

Part Three

Chapter Sixteen
Courtship, Marriage and Family Life

It was a love affair that began one balmy, late summer Sunday evening in 1929 and lasted over sixty years. Woodrow Melvin met Juanita Weekes at the First Baptist church youth fellowship the night before he entered his senior year in Milton High School.

The words of the speaker at the front of the church fell on deaf ears as far as Woodrow was concerned; his concentration was on the tall, slim, attractive brunette who sat with a group of teenage girls a few rows ahead of him.

Finally, Woodrow could stand it no longer and he leaned over to one of his pals and whispered, "Billy, who's the new girl in town?"

"Nita Weekes. Comes from Jay. At least that's what my sister told me. Parents are down here to teach school. She's caught your eye, has she, Woodie?" Billy gave his friend his aah-haa smile. "Can't deny, she's pretty."

Woodrow's face felt warm and flushed. "I just want to meet her, o.k.?"

"Well, when you talk to her see if she's got a sister." Billy's chuckle caught the attention of the speaker and for the remainder of the sermon the man didn't take his eyes off the back pew.

Woodrow took advantage of the time for refreshments to make his acquaintance. With a cool glass of lemonade in each hand he walked up to Nita and welcomed her to Milton.

"Are you anxious to start classes tomorrow?" he asked.

"A little. I've never been to a school this big; I hope I find the right rooms."

Woodrow smiled. "Not to worry, Nita; we're a friendly group. We'll head you in the right direction."

Nita's uneasiness weighed on Woodrow's mind all the way home and before his eyes closed for the night, he'd made a decision. At dawn's first light, he jumped out of bed, readied himself for school, ate a bowl of grits and was standing at the curb in front of Nita's house before any of the other boys found her. He considered it his duty to personally escort this girl to her new school.

As the year progressed, their lives became more and more entwined; they participated in musical productions, debates, sports, clubs and parties. But before they knew it, graduation separated them and Woodrow enrolled in Pensacola Business School.

During the second half of Nita's senior year, Woodrow began his work in the typing pool in Tallahassee for the legislative session. Determined to win his high school sweetheart, he resorted to an unusual plan to keep her attention.

A look of endearment comes over Nita's face as the telling of the memory resurfaces.

"I was taking Algebra 2 under Creary Hamilton and every morning about nine or ten o'clock this boy walks up and bangs on the door. Mr. Hamilton goes over to the door and takes a registered telegram addressed to Juanita Weekes from Woodrow Melvin in Tallahassee. I got one every day. I never knew what the teacher thought but he'd just call me to come sign for it and I'd go back to my seat. Of course, I couldn't read it in class; I'd have to wait."

One such telegram, delivered for Valentine's Day, expressed poetically the love Woodrow felt for Nita: "I HAVE NO HEART TO SEND YOU FOR I WOULD HAVE YOU KNOW THE

ONLY ONE I EVER HAD I GAVE YOU LONG AGO"
WOODROW

There were further separations, for after Nita's graduation, as Woodrow returned to Milton to work as time keeper on the highway project, Nita arrived in Tallahassee to attend Florida State College for Women in pursuit of a teaching degree. After two years, she accepted a position teaching in Munson. By this time, Woodrow was ready to attend law school in Tennessee. Distance, however, was not a detriment in the blossoming relationship. To show Nita's parents that his intentions were honorable, Woodrow sent them a letter.

Dear Mr. Weekes,

As it may be several weeks before Nita returns home and I will have an opportunity to talk with you, I am writing you concerning the plans that we have made for our future. When you and I were discussing this matter some several days ago, I told you that when we had decided upon our plans definitely, I would outline them to you in detail.

Since our conversation, Nita and I have thoroughly discussed the matter and concluded this to be our program. We plan for her to teach school in Munson for the ensuing term while I am in Cumberland University. I expect to be there but one term. I shall take the bar examination given after I return from Cumberland—and it is then that we plan to marry. I have asked, and she has agreed to wait for me.

Mr. Weekes, I more than appreciate the many courtesies that you have extended to me and it is my determination never to give you cause to regret having done so.

Sincerely yours,
Woodrow

With each letter or telegram Nita received from her beloved, her heart ached. She longed to be with him and the feeling was mutual. By Christmas holidays, they decided to start off the New Year as husband and wife.

"Woodrow," Nita said, "I'm satisfied to get married in my parent's home. Now that they've moved to Tallahassee there won't be many family members attending. It'll be a small affair but I need to give Mama at least a day's notice to bake a cake."

"Didn't you tell me she's driving over to Milton for some Womens' Club meeting tomorrow?"

"I'm sure that's what her letter told me. Lucky for us we can get a ride back with her and not have to take the train."

Delighted to hear her daughter's plans, Mrs. Weekes insisted they leave immediately after she'd concluded her business.

By the time they arrived in the capital it was 2:00 a.m. but Nita bounded up the steps, waking her father. "Daddy! Daddy! We've got news. There's going to be a wedding! Woodrow and I are getting married."

Mr. Weekes rolled over in his bed, opened one eye and said, "Well, you can't do it tonight. Do you think you can wait until tomorrow afternoon when I get up?"

With that he smiled, held out his arms and gave his daughter a huge hug.

The following day, Woodrow paid $2.50 for the marriage license that Nita's parents had to sign since she was not yet twenty-one. Next, they arranged for the pastor of the First Presbyterian Church to marry them at the Weekes home that evening. When time came for the ceremony, the guests arrived, the bride and groom were ready, but there was no clergy. After forty-five minutes someone knocked on the door.

"Well, finally," sighed Nita. "Daddy, can you let him in?"

Mr. Weekes opened the door and to the amazement of everyone, there stood the Reverend in overalls and rubber boots.

"Good evening, sir. Could you tell me what time tomorrow I'm to perform the wedding?"

"Now," said Woodrow and Nita in unison. "Come on in. We're all ready."

The Reverend's face turned pale and he apologized repeatedly as he wiped at his attire. "I'm so sorry dear folks, but if you'll give me half an hour I'll be cleaned up and back before you know it."

Sure to his word, the next knock on the door opened to a suit-clad, spiffed-up, pastor carrying the word of God in his hand.

There was no honeymoon trip. The next day, with seven dollars between them, they boarded the Greyhound bus together but even this trip did not last long. Woodrow had to change buses in Marianna to go back to college and Nita had to complete her teaching term in Munson. Not a typical start to wedded bliss but it was the beginning of a marriage that lasted sixty-years.

***

Nita knew from the beginning that in order to be a supportive wife to Woodrow her role would constantly change. Whether it meant packing up and moving to Tallahassee for periods of time, staying home to care for their children, working in the law office or providing impromptu lunches to the folks Woodrow invited home from the courthouse, she did it in stride. Her personal commitment to the marriage ran deep. When asked the secret to keeping their relationship strong, she was not hesitant to reply, "I think it was because we decided in the beginning that was what we wanted to do. And we just did it; you don't ever think about not doing it once you make up your mind."

Woodrow added, "My wife has influenced me the most; every time I said I couldn't do something, she believed I could. It all worked out fine. She's my partner.

A moment of unspoken tenderness passed between husband and wife and he continued, "She probably didn't get her fair share; maybe we'll get it straightened out before the trip's over."

When called upon as judge to perform a marriage ceremony, Woodrow took it seriously and wrote his own script based on the philosophy that had worked for him and Nita over the years. It read:

"Nothing is easier than saying words. Nothing is harder than living them day after day. What you promise today must be renewed and re-decided tomorrow and each day that stretches out before you.

"At the end of this ceremony legally you will be man and wife, but still you must decide each day that you want to be married. All of us know you are deeply in love. But beyond the warmth and the glow, the excitement and romance, what is love really?

"Real love is not total absorption in each other; it is looking outward in the same direction—together.

"Love makes burdens lighter, because you divide them. It makes joys more intense because you share them. It makes you stronger, so that you can reach out and become involved with life in ways you dared not risk alone.

"The ring of precious metal has forever been the symbol of marriage. The precious metal typifying purity and worth and the ring being without end symbolizing the eternal duration of this relationship.

"We have heard you promise to share your lives in marriage. We recognize and respect the covenants you have made. It is not a judge standing before you that makes your marriage real, but the honesty and sincerity of what you have said and done here before your family and friends and in the sight of God. On behalf of all those present, I acknowledge that you are husband and wife."

With every couple who stood before Judge Melvin and participated in a marriage ceremony, Woodrow prayed they would take his words in earnest and he wouldn't have to meet them again in divorce court.

"I've seen a lot of marriages hit the rocks. I am of the opinion that many of them are entered into without real consideration of the consequences—haven't given it the place in their thinking that it is entitled too—instead of a serious holy arrangement, it's thought of as a flippant thing. If it doesn't work, we'll just go by and get a divorce. If it costs more to get married than to get a divorce, maybe that might help the situation. But then again, if people aren't going to live together, I guess there's some good to be said for Florida's 'no fault' divorce system. That at lest cuts down on a lot of perjury.

"If grown people come into court and say they don't want to live together anymore, they can pretty quick get a divorce. But if there's children, therein is the tragedy. Of course, the court gives consideration to the children but that's not sufficient. A child doesn't only need the mama. They need the daddy and the mama living together in some state of harmony so that the child can have a well-rounded view of life as it develops. There's not the understanding like there used to be."

***

Having been raised in homes that knew the laughter and tears of siblings, both Woodrow and Nita were anxious to start their own family. For quite some time, it looked as if it might not happen. They made the decision to start adoption proceedings but, to their delight, nature took its course and in their sixth year of marriage, they became parents to Woodrow(Mac) Jr. born September 18, 1941. For the next fourteen years, the Melvin household continued to grow.

A second son, Samuel James, was born February 26, 1945; a daughter, Laura Nita, arrived February 21,1947, a second daughter, Beulah Evans joined the family in November 23,1950 and the youngest, another daughter, Esther Virginia was welcomed October 22,1955.

As the years passed, eight grandchildren grew in the love of their grandparents. Woodrow, with his innate ability to put things into perspective, expressed a humorous sentiment when the grandkids came to call:

"The headlights on the car sure looked good comin' but by the end of the evening, the taillights looked even better."

Parents: Laura and David

June, 1940
Sons of Laura and David Melvin
Left to right: Hiram (Mac), Joe, George, John, Woodrow, Perry

April 1974
Left to right: Perry, Woodrow, John, George, Joe, Hiram (Mac)

Woodrow Melvin – Milton High School Senior, 1929

Woodrow Melvin – 1931

Newlyweds:
Woodrow and Nita, January 1, 1935

Woodrow with sons Mac and Jim

Beulah, Laura, Ginger, Jim and Mac

Woodrow and Nita's
25th Wedding Anniversary

Celebrating 50 Golden Years

Woodrow celebrates his 80th birthday with family,
December 16, 1992

Chapter Seventeen
Intimate Insights

Woodrow Melvin stands favorably in the eyes of the public. The decisions he made and the laws he helped write retain implications that affect their lives. But at the end of the day's work, when he put down the gavel and took off the black robe, what kind of man came home for supper? What influence did he wield in his children's lives? What advice did he offer them? What memories did he imprint in their minds? For answers to these questions, it is best to listen to the words of his children.

Laura, his eldest daughter voices positive memories, even though her father was gone from home a great deal of the time. "Daddy," she recalls, "had a beautiful singing voice and loved to whistle, especially, if he was in a joyful mood.

"Along with Mother, he fostered a sense of independence early in my life. Daddy knew I wasn't one to play with dolls and he replaced that by buying me a gun and holster set just like my big brothers. He also bought me a zippered jacket with a rabbit collar. I thought it was special but by the look on Mother's face I knew she would have preferred a little more feminine style.

"There was never any challenge my parents presented to me that I thought I couldn't do. One summer when I was six they allowed me to take the train from Milton to Tallahassee by myself to meet Daddy when he was in the Senate. I didn't have enough sense to be afraid. Mother gave me to a conductor who watched over me and helped me change trains in Marianna where another conductor took charge. I had a high time; I thought it was wonderful. The tethers have always been long even when it came to a six-year-old taking a solo train trip. They knew exactly what was happening and where I was at all times.

"This attitude my parents taught us that we *could do* whatever it was that we were looking at made a big impact on my future decisions; there wasn't much energy spent on the *why you can't*. Sometimes if we were getting to the place where they were getting nervous about what we were doing they might get quiet but they didn't berate it. We've done some interesting things because they helped us believe that we could. They trusted our instincts and by putting the onus on us to make responsible choices it shaped our character. Now, we didn't always like it and my sister Ginger flatly stated that she'd have much rather heard mom or dad tell her that she couldn't do something then tell her they trusted her judgment.

"The time I spent working in Daddy's office gave me the opportunity to see another dimension of his personality. I was familiar with his gentleness, his humor and his intelligence, but in this public arena I saw a man who had the ability to be forceful in a quiet and diplomatic way. He could look someone in the eye and come across like cold steel because that's what it took to get the job done. He needed this trait because as Chairman of the Qualifications Commission, he had to go behind closed doors and convince a judge to resign in order to avoid what would happen to him if he refused.

"Of course, living in a small town with a high profile parent is not much different from being a preacher's kid. Sometimes I felt as though I was growing up in a fishbowl. Other people made a lot of it but Daddy didn't.

"He never said, 'Don't you do that, you'll embarrass me.' Nothing of that sort ever came from him but in the community I was looked at as the judge's daughter. The expectations were higher.

140

When I think about the years my parents spent together I realize that they were never programmed to get divorced. There's nothing that would have caused them to separate. They had their fair share of problems, some very big ones, but they were blessed to be in a relationship where they liked each other.

"They gave each other strength. Dad did real well *'out there'* but when it came into the circle of the family he could be like jello. He didn't have the same strengths that he had dealing with the outside. Mom was like steel and he relied on her for some of that strength as she stood beside him. It was a true partnership. That song 'Wind Beneath My Wings' at the very least was what she was to him."

"Daddy's vulnerability may have shown itself at home, but when it came to the courtroom there was no doubt who was in control—especially the lawyers. Because of conflict of interest, I was never able to practice in his court, but I watched as he respectfully prodded the respective parties to get to the bottom line.

"One time I watched a lawyer who did not 'cut to the chase' and proceedings were lagging behind. Daddy began to squirm a little and at the first opportunity he looked at the lawyer, motioned for him to come forward and said, "You have ploughed that furrow several times; please move on to the next."

When I became a judge, one of my favorite times with my father was discussing in theoretical terms some case. We never talked about specifics as that was not ethical but all I had to say was, 'Let me run this one by you' and his face lit up and I knew I had his attention. Since law was a common interest for us, our communication grew.

"One of my proudest memories concerning our appreciation for the law involved a trip to the U.S. Supreme Court in Washington, D.C. where my brother, Mac, argued a case there. Dad and I got to sit, not in the public gallery, but in the special area reserved for those attorneys who have applied and been admitted to argue before the U.S. Supreme Court. It was such a big deal to me to sit with him in that esteemed place. Mac lost his argument but it was still a great day!

"I realize as time goes by that a person's name is a temporal thing. Daddy will be remembered as a judge with an even temperament who was fair. He was much more but I don't know that the reality of time will hold more than that."

***

Jim, the second eldest son, a retired Air Force Colonel and C.P.A., reflects on his relationship with his father from a male perspective.

"As a youngster growing up, I remember Daddy as a warm and thoughtful person who had a passion for practicing law and getting involved in politics. Both endeavors took a lot of his time and during the week he often worked late. I looked forward to the week-ends though because I knew he'd probably take me and my brother fishing. He taught us how to throw a net but I never did pick up his expertise. At night we'd go fish for flounder, too.

"Daddy encouraged me as I grew older to 'keep my inventory between my ears', in other words to educate myself. For instance, while Daddy was in the Senate, I got my first paying job at an early age working as a page in the House of Representatives for John Pitman, who was the representative who took Dad's chair in the House. It was a fun job and I got a first hand look at what my father did over there in Tallahassee.

"Our home was like any other that had teenage boys. There were times when a firm but loving hand was needed. Dad had such a soft spoken approach to discipline. He could talk to you and make you feel terrible about what you'd done. If you really got him angry with you, he would become very soft spoken—the softer the tone, the harder you better listen because you could coax him into dusting your britches; he was not opposed to corporal punishment. He just didn't resort to it very often.

"A lesson in life he taught me was that a man's word was his bond. I learned that if you told my father you would do something, then it had better get done.

"One day he came home and saw that the grass was not cut. I had told him in the morning that I would do it. Our conversation went something like this:

"'Now, son,' he said, 'you know a man's word is his bond; you told me you were going to mow the yard. You didn't tell me you were going to do half of it; you didn't tell me you were going to do it as long as you wanted to do it and when you got tired you were going to quit. You told me that you were going to mow the yard, didn't you, son?'

"'Yes, sir, Daddy, I told you I would mow the yard.'

"'I asked you if you would mow the yard and you said you would mow the yard, is that not correct?'

"'Yes, sir, that's right.'

"'You didn't tell me you would mow until the guys wanted you to go swimmin' and then quit.'

"'No, sir, I told you'"

"That was his approach to discipline and to life itself. It was an attitude that followed me into my military career.

"I never thought it unusual that most folks in town knew who my father was. There was just one time while I was growing up that Dad's name and the fact that I was a judge's son give me any grief. Another judge in the area had a son that got into trouble with the law and the rumor mill tagged me as the culprit until the situation got resolved.

"When I look back on my father's political career, I believe it was a public service or calling as strong as any spiritual leader might feel. It cost him money to be in the legislature because he was away from his law practice and it didn't pay a salary except for an expense account of $6.50 a day.

"It took me a while to understand that while Dad was in the legislature he could oppose someone without being their enemy. As a young person, I observed people on the opposite side of Dad politically that he held in high esteem. In my mind, that was a mixed message and it baffled me.

"The Governor of the State of Florida was a guy named Leroy Collins. And daddy and Leroy didn't get along in my childish mind, when in fact, daddy had the utmost respect for the man. Leroy was a different cut of political cloth but he was an honest, solid, public serving politician whose political views

143

weren't the same as my father's. They could agree to disagree—and did. And charged each other for those disagreements. It was like pulling teeth for Leroy Collins to get things through the Senate. There was a long stretch of time when not one shovel of slag was thrown or one inch of road repaired in northwest Florida in retaliation because the governor could cause that not to happen. There was a price to pay and Dad was a very conservative thinker.

"One aspect of Dad's compassionate nature that was private and he did not put on public display was his financial support to children's charities. I personally saw that the cliché, actions speak louder than words, applied to my father.

"He never passed a Shriner on the street without putting something in the bucket and he raised us to help the Shriners. He was very proud of what they did; especially the burn hospitals and the fact that nobody who needed help was ever charged a penny.

"He also was a quiet supporter of orphanages; there was one in Mexico where he knew the set-up, knew the people, and knew that the finances were not being consumed as they trickled through the organization as so often happens. He had no patience at all for these situations where you give a dollar and a nickel of it goes to actually help someone.

"Of all the obstacles, challenges, problems and decisions Dad had to face in his lifetime, nothing was more frustrating than the dimming effect the diabetes had on his eyesight. His eyes were one of the most important tools of his trade. He felt as though he was a forty-year old man trapped in an eighty-year old body. At this stage of his life, he had no choice but to rest his case."

***

Beulah, a middle child, has vague memories of her father beginning his career as a judge. She remembers living the first few years of her life in the family homestead on Berryhill Street then moving to the new house on Blackwater Bay.

"Daddy always had time for everyone's questions and I know that the community was important to him and consequently anytime someone requested information of him he was more than willing to give it. He didn't mean to focus so much attention away from the family at that time—it just happened. There were always people around though. I remember fondly the summer evening campfires beside the bay with friends.

"Only once do I remember traveling on a vacation with my parents. Ginger and I went out to California with mom and daddy. We had a grand time in the back of a Ford Fairlane going across the desert. Daddy really didn't like to go too far from Milton so they stayed close to home most of the time.

"When it came time to make a career decision, I knew I wanted to take a different course than my elder sister and brother who chose law. I leaned toward my mother's vocation and went into teaching. I received my B.A. in Early Childhood Education as well as a Masters degree in both Business and School Administration.

"Daddy never tried to steer me in any particular direction; I was free to choose. The best advice he could give me was not the spoken word but his own behavior modeling. I learned a lot watching him; I learned that people are people no matter how important they are. We saw many people come and go through our house—a lot of Senators and Representatives but each were treated exactly the same as the person down the road who was a neighbor or just happened to be an acquaintance Daddy knew. He treated everyone with the same respect unless you didn't deserve it and then he was never rude about it but was very cool and reserved.

"I think some people within our small community had some ideas about our family. I think they thought we were much better off financially than, in fact, we were and they felt the contacts with the outside world were bigger than they were. In some instances I was miscast in high school but that was just part of the growing process and I think I benefited from it in the long run. It certainly helped me to identify people's thoughts and traits based on opinion rather than on fact. So I guess I was treated both positively and negatively because he was my father.

"I'm not sure that the community expected more or less of me but I liked the idea that mom and dad expected me to do well at whatever I tried and I never wanted to disappoint them. I was always proud of daddy but I never wore it as a badge. Any door he may have opened for me was an opening and then it was my job and responsibility to walk on through and do the best I could. Daddy would have been extremely upset had I tried to behave in any other fashion and pretend as though because he was my dad I didn't have to do what had to be done.

"I believe my father was a brilliant man with a tremendous amount of education without being an overly educated man. His greatest sorrow was that he did not have as much college education as his children but he was proud of what we had. He valued education highly and I knew as a young child that it was very important. If I can pass along to my children the same level of education that my parents passed along to me then I feel like I will have joined the 'circle of life'. That is one of the biggest contributions my father made in my life and will continue to make through his grandchildren."

***

In the following 1994 eulogy, Mac, the eldest son, a lawyer in Miami, expressed his admiration for his father through the heritage Woodrow brought to the family.

"Dad's ancestral origins were humble. As best we know, Dad's great-great-great-great grandfather was Irish. He swam ashore, literally a 'wet-back', and settled in Baden County, North Carolina in the 1500's. His name was David Melvin. Apparently, David had been enroute to America when his ship was seized by Blackbeard the Pirate, and David was taken captive. Somewhere off shore of Baden County, North Carolina, David and some friends escaped over the side and swam to America.

"By the time of the Civil War, Dad's Irish ancestors had migrated south. His great-great grandfather David, was killed by a Yankee soldier and lies buried on the banks of the Yellow River near Holt.

"We also know that his Irish blood was mixed with some Scottish genes, and that Dad's paternal grandmother, Mary Melvin, was a full-blooded Choctaw Indian. Her family was from the Florida panhandle. In that respect, it might be said that some of the blood in Dad's veins came from the deepest and least understood history of this great country, for fully one-quarter of it was American Indian.

"His parents, David and Laura Melvin, were hard working and not well off financially. Dad's father worked in a sawmill somewhere on the Yellow River in Santa Rosa County until he was a grown man of twenty-one years. Barefoot and illiterate, he walked into Milton looking for a better life. Soon enough, David Melvin learned to read and write better than most others in town. Eventually, he became the town clerk and then the County Tax Assessor. Dad always had the deepest respect for his own father's humble origins.

"Dad believed that the practice of law was one of man's noblest endeavors. And, the way he practiced law, it was. His practice did very well, as did his political ambitions. He served as Mayor of the town of Milton and then was elected to the Florida House of Representatives.

"Woodrow's love of public service carried him to major accomplishments. As a member of the legislature, he wrote the first law in Florida to require that every school child be provided a hot lunch, whether the parents could afford to pay for it or not. He believed that a hungry child was disadvantaged unfairly compared to a well fed one.

"He introduced the legislative bill that created Pensacola College. To him, education was "real" personal power. It was freedom. Education was the key to the future for all diligent enough to pursue it. He believed it was one of the government's wisest investments in its citizens.

"He sat among the lofty membership of the Florida Senate and counted nearly every Senator as his friend. Later, as a judge, he would sit as the first chairman of the Qualifications

Committee and eventually, Dad was offered a prestigious judgeship on the First District Court of Appeals of Florida.

"In 1979, Dad retired from the appellate court in Tallahassee and from full time judicial service. As he entered the winter of his years, Dad spent more time with his now very large extended family and with his beloved Juanita. The days grew short and became a special few. But his days were happy, his health generally good. Philosophically, Dad knew that every season must end, and that every living thing must someday die.

"This truth was, in Dad's opinion, the simple and elegant process Mother Nature uses to make the "old" move out and let the "new" move in. He had no illusions about the finality of this process, and regarded it as a merciful and proper conclusion to life on this earth.

"One of Dad's favorite prayers simply said:

"'God grant me the serenity to accept the things I cannot change,

'The courage to change the things I can,

'And the wisdom to know the difference.'

"Dad, we all loved you and you loved us. Now, you have started a new journey. Our final wish for you was composed long ago by the old Irish poet who wrote:

"'May the road rise to meet you,

May the sun shine warm upon your face,

The rains fall soft upon your fields,

Until we meet again,

May God hold you in the palm of His hand.'

"Godspeed, Daddy. And thank you for everything."

Woodrow and son Mac, also a lawyer,
standing on the steps of the
U.S. Supreme Court, Washington, D.C.

Part Four

Chapter Eighteen
A Word from His Friends

The love Woodrow Melvin had for people on all levels was evident by a simple salute of his hat, to engaging in the most intense, personal conversation.

Scores of individuals walked through his life, each one touched in a special way; but there were some who had daily contact, such as court clerks, secretaries, attorneys, and judges.

Judge George Lowery, now deceased, once recounted the years he practiced law in Judge Melvin's courtroom then worked with him on the bench as a colleague.

"In 1963, I came to Milton and started practicing law. As a young lawyer, I appreciated the way Judge Melvin helped novice attorneys and I followed his example when I became a judge.

"I recall a divorce case I filed for a lady whose husband had moved off to Alabama and he wouldn't support her or the kids. She didn't feel she would be able to enforce alimony and what she really wanted was the farm. We had to serve him by publication we took a default as he didn't answer to the complaint. When I took the matter to Judge Melvin for the final hearing he looked through the file and said, In the type of proceeding that you are following here I notice that you haven't set out the legal description of the property in your notice of suit. While you've given him notice of the pending suit, you probably need to include it in order to insure that you won't have to come back and clear a title later."

"It was very helpful as a young attorney without an older attorney in my office to discuss those kind of matters. It was a mistake that was caught at the time to save some litigation later on.

"On another occasion, I was defending an action for a gentleman who was intent on preventing this property owner from getting ingress and egress across a piece of land and there were some technical deficiencies in the complaint that was filed. I moved to dismiss and Judge Melvin granted the motion. They amended the complaint and we came back a second time and I filed another motion to dismiss which he granted. They amended a third time and I filed another motion to dismiss and the judge, instead of granting it this time, instructed the attorney what he specifically needed to allege and put in his complaint. Afterwards Judge Melvin said to me, 'George, he'll stumble up on the right way to do this eventually anyway, but the litigation is really that of the client's and he needs to have his day in court and get heard; so I'm going to help him get these technicalities out of the way where we can get on with this litigation.'

"Judge Melvin brought a sense of humanity to the bench. He was in touch with reality and what was going on. He never used an ivory tower approach. He was a country judge who understood people extremely well and could apply the law to them as they were—fallible humans. He was able to maintain the dignity and respect for the court while being less formal than one or two of the judges in Pensacola. While he treated people with cordiality, warmth and humanness, he still maintained control of his courtroom.

"Now, he could get somebody straight if need be; he didn't tolerate anything improper or inappropriate. He also didn't like big city lawyers to come over and act patronizing toward him.

"I recall once that I was working as co-counsel with one of the local bank attorneys on a claim against an insurance

154

company. The bank had loaned money to a fellow to purchase an aircraft and naturally they required that it be insured and that the insurance be payable to the bank as long as there was an outstanding lien.

"The fellow did not have a commercial license and was not supposed to be flying anyone for hire, however, he did and got into a storm, crashed the plane and everyone was killed. The insurance company refused to pay the bank. They hired a firm to represent them out of Jacksonville rather than employing one in Pensacola. The lawyer flew over and filed a motion to dismiss the case. We were in Judge Melvin's chambers and since the moving party on the motion goes first, this attorney was explaining his position about why we weren't entitled to maintain this suit. He kept referring to a copy of a policy he had taken from his file and was really making some comments that were patronizing to Judge Melvin as though Woodrow wouldn't understand.

"He'd say, 'Judge, this is a contract; you see, a contract is an agreement between the parties and they are bound by the terms and conditions of it.'

"This attorney was older; he wasn't a young attorney who didn't know any better and after about the third time, Judge Melvin reached over and gently tapped the policy laying on the table. He looked directly at the man and responded in that quiet, steady voice, 'I think you can assume that I've read two or three of these in my time and you don't need to make that point again.'

"He heard a little more then he continued, 'Well, I think you've had a reasonable opportunity to make your point and you don't have anything here that warrants this motion to be filed; it's rather frivolous so the motion to dismiss is denied and you'll file your answer in ten days.'"

Judge Lowery continued to praise his mentor.

"I always appreciated the fact that Judge Melvin was predictable. The same factual circumstance would get the same result regardless of who the litigant was. It's nice to know that when you go before a judge that you can base the advice to your client on what you understand the law to be and know that the judge is first and foremost going to apply that law and follow it and not decide the case on partiality.

"Another trait I admired about Woodrow was his informal approach to the issues of a case. If it were necessary to bring the lawyers into his chambers he would begin by asking each party, 'Now, what is your understanding of the situation that we are going to be dealing with here?' One side would explain; the other would comment and Woodrow might say, 'Well, you know, I don't think that dog will hunt.'"

A smile preceded Judge Lowery's comment. "It was not a typical response that one might hear in a more authoritative, reserved court elsewhere in the state. It did, however, work for this Circuit Court judge.

"In 1979, when Woodrow returned from Tallahassee and began re-call work, our friendship grew stronger. Many times we used each other as sounding boards over a cup of coffee to discuss a particular point of law pertinent to a pending case. Indirectly, it was time well spent not only for us but for the parties involved.

"On more than one occasion, Woodrow commented to me that while in Tallahassee he missed the day-to-day court activity with the attorneys. After a case had been argued before the Appellate Court, the lawyers felt it inappropriate to come back and visit. I really believe the best thing Woodrow could have done was come back to Santa Rosa County to work part-time.

"I'm not one given to the adulation complex we seem to have in this country over sports figures, politicians, presidents or anything else. They just don't impress me. But I think I knew Woodrow Melvin well enough to have known his character, moral fiber and the kind of person he was that set him above and apart virtually from anybody I've known.

"If the Lord said to me, "We made a mistake and your father cannot be your father, you'll have to pick somebody else. Woodrow is the one person that would come to mind. I thought the world of him."

***

156

Administrative Assistants: Kathy and Jeanelle

The fact that litigation in Judge Melvin's courtroom ran in a smooth efficient manner was evident in the co-operative teamwork done by his assistants—Kathy Jordan and Jeanelle Kingry. They handled the continuous stream of paperwork, constant phone calls and changing schedules.

Kathy's eyes grew misty and her voice softened. "He never treated us like employees. He was like family and he made you feel special so you wanted to do your best. I miss him so much. Something has been lost since the older judges have left the bench.

"If there was an error in scheduling, it could have been my error but he would never acknowledge that I could possibly have made a mistake. He'd just tell me it was all right and have the attorneys reschedule.

"Even the Chief Judge knew how Judge Melvin treated his staff. I was told that my name came up and that the senior judge stated, 'She's the best protected judicial assistant in the system. I considered that a compliment.'

"The few times I saw Judge Melvin upset involved the abuse or neglect of children. Sometimes, even in divorce cases, he could see the child's pain and it bothered him. Domestic cases were always the hardest for him to do.

"This concern for family came first in our office. If I had to leave early to attend to one of my children, there was never any conflict. He was compassionate of the working mother and always told me, 'Go; take care of the children and don't worry about this place.'

Jeanelle, also a court reporter, saw Woodrow as he interacted with different parties in the courtroom. Her eyes observed a judge who was in control and very straightforward—never wishy-washy or evasive. He saw through the rhetoric and got to the heart of the matter.

One time, she and Woodrow were sitting in the courtroom as observers while another judge presided over a first degree murder case. Jeanelle recalled the situation:

"A man had been sleeping at a rest area on Interstate 10. He was robbed, taken out of the car, dragged out into the woods, tied to a tree and then shot in the head. It was a horrible murder. The defendant was found guilty and the decision was being made to give him life or death. In the closing arguments, the defense attorney brought in a metronome and let it tick off forty seconds. He claimed it took as much as forty seconds or longer to kill someone in the electric chair. The testimony in the trial stated that when the man was shot in the head he died instantly. The attorney went on to argue that it would be so brutal to sentence this man to die in the electric chair when it might take as long as a minute to kill him, whereas, his client was more merciful by shooting the fellow in the head.

"Judge Melvin leaned over to me and said, 'I've never heard of shooting someone in the head as mercy killing. Perhaps they should give him a choice; shoot him in the head or electrocute him.'"

Jeanelle further explained, "In Judge Melvin's courtroom, he realized that jurors, especially in a first degree murder case, must make a recommendation that could mean life or death for another human being. He was always sensitive to their feelings and many times I heard him express to the jury the court's gratitude for their time, the recommendation they made, but most important, he wanted them to understand that now they could forget it. The final decision was on his shoulders and they need not look back and wonder if they did the right thing.

"I do remember a humorous situation that once again showed Judge Melvin's ability to communicate with people whatever the circumstance.

"A black lady came in with her daughter who was about seventeen and very pregnant. She wanted to talk to the judge because the hospital was telling her that unless she paid up front she couldn't check in and have her baby there. The baby was due in a week and she was all upset.

"I kept telling her that the judge was busy and that she'd need to talk to someone else since it really wasn't something a judge would be involved with. She wouldn't leave, so finally I went in and told Judge Melvin what she wanted. He walked to the door, acknowledged her and went on to say, 'I'll tell you what to do; I can't order the hospital to treat your daughter but when you know that it's time for her to have that baby, you take her to the hospital just like you normally would and you tell them that she's here to have the baby. If they won't check her in, then just go in the lobby, let her lie on the couch and they'll see that she gets to the right place.'

"That lady was so satisfied it was like he had solved all her problems. I never did know what happened in the end.

"I'll never forget one of the first depositions Judge Melvin asked me to take for a contested divorce hearing. It had come up unexpectedly and I needed to locate a shorthand pad and a recorder. Woodrow advised the attorneys that it would be about fifteen minutes before things got started.

"I ran frantically around to each office in the courthouse hunting, but could not find a tape recorder. Giving up, I returned to Judge Melvin's office to face the music without one. 'Judge, I'm not sure I can handle this.'

"Woodrow saw my shaking hands. 'Sit down, Jeanelle. Relax. I'm going to take care of this.'

"With a quick wink he continued, 'How many times have you heard me say: *all things work out if you live right?*'

"I sat down but I certainly didn't relax. I could hardly breathe; I was frightened to face the lawyers. Eventually, T.Sol Johnson and David Levin came in and informed us that while they were waiting on me to find a tape recorder, they had settled the case and needed only to dictate a stipulation into the record. Judge Melvin looked over at me and smiled. What a relief. He was indeed a unique gentleman."

***

Ray Helms
County Clerk

January 9, 1957, is a special date for Ray Helms. Not only

was it the day Woodrow took the bench, but it was the same day Ray became County Clerk. For the next twenty years, these two men worked hand in hand. Ray recalled one incident at the beginning of their working relationship that put things right on track.

"A good friend of mine was getting a divorce and the guy asked me to talk to Judge Melvin to see if he'd go easy on the settlement. Of course, here I go, only in office six months, and say, 'Judge, you got a divorce coming up and if there's any way you can go easy on the man, he'd appreciate it.'"

"Judge Melvin looked at me and said, 'Let me make a deal with you.' I thought to myself that I had it made. He raised his glasses, looked at me, and said, 'The deal is—you be the clerk and let me be the judge.'"

"I got the message and from then on a bond of friendship grew between us that was as close as father and son. If I had a problem, I could go to him for advice and he didn't mind talking to me because the better job I did, the better it was for him since we did all the legal work for the court. I traveled the circuit with him and went to all the conferences. "There won't ever be one like him; he used a common sense approach to judging and he was never too busy to shake someone's hand, either. We'd be in the courthouse corridors and some fella would come in dressed in dirty work clothes, could have been a farmer or some type of laborer. Judge Melvin would speak to him and shake hands. I'd ask him if he knew that person and he'd say, 'Well, I know he's a citizen of this county and he's a voter. You got to treat them just like you do that fella with the coat and tie because they'll go to the polls and vote.'"

Ray chuckled as he recounted the time Woodrow decided to quit smoking cigars and a pipe.

"Since I was also a smoker, it meant less time for me to indulge in the habit. While we were in the courtroom, I always kept water on the bench for him. But when he quit smoking, I made sure that his glass was never empty. He would drink so much he would have to take a bathroom break and I could smoke. After about a month he caught on to what I was doing and he

160

called me over to the bench and whispered, 'I know how to swear in a witness, I know the oath, I don't need you up here and I can pour my own damn water. You want to smoke; just go smoke.'"

"As a former teacher, I appreciated the practice Woodrow had of allowing visiting school classes to come into court while he was in session to observe the judicial system at work. After the students were seated, he would tell the attorneys and the jury that they were going to stop the proceedings for a few minutes. Everyone stayed in the courtroom while Judge Melvin recognized the teachers and students. It made them feel special as he talked to them and often would have the State Attorney and Public Defender explain their different roles. These field trips left an impression on many a young mind.

"I feel that the residents of Santa Rosa County will remember an intelligent, compassionate, common sense kind of man. Always aware of his timing, Judge Melvin knew when to step down from the bench."

***

Butch Lindsay
Attorney

When Butch Lindsay started practicing law in Judge Melvin's courtroom, he was no stranger to Woodrow. As a child, Butch remembers being marched down to the Melvin household to face the consequences of a boyish prank he, Jim and Mac Jr. had participated in.

"One day we were swimming in a little water hole down by Alabama Street, about where the Garden Center is now, and one of us got the idea to shoot moons at the passing motorists. We were happily engaged in that activity when one of the motorist happened to be a member of the police department. We were escorted down the street about a block to Woodrow's house. Well, when he got finished telling me all I'd done, I'd wished he'd whipped me.

"I really got to know him from the years I spent as a

161

prosecuting attorney trying cases in Judge Melvin's courtroom. George Phillips from the Public Defender's office, and I had a way of telling how many years a man was going to get in prison by how red Woodrow's head would get. If Woodrow ever had hair on the top of his head, I don't remember it; but as he discussed with the defendant what he had done and how he was going to be treated by the judiciary, we were pretty certain if Woodrow's head got a little bit red the man was going to have to spend some county jail time and maybe even some state time. In cases of armed robbery or heinous crimes, his whole head would start getting red at the front and gradually move right on to the back. If Judge Melvin was going to send you away for a long time, you couldn't tell it by his voice because he was always so calm and easy going and even real nice to the criminal. For a while, until one of us noticed, there was absolutely no way to know what was going on but when we started seeing his head light up, we joked in the halls that we knew the guy was going to get ten years.

"As an attorney, I respected the efficiently run courtroom but also the high standards he expected from the lawyers who came before him. I don't know of any judge before whom I have practiced who not only expected more from a lawyer but *taught* more to a lawyer. He demanded that you be courteous, respectful, know what you were talking about and be prepared. Some of us messed up and weren't prepared; that happens because of scheduling or perhaps the lawyer is not motivated for one reason or another. He would let you know in a way that made you better prepared the next time.

"One attorney who learned this lesson was a man who was notorious for being absent in court if he wasn't ready. Brooks Taylor was one of the finest criminal defense lawyers in this part of the country during a time when he was working hard and not physically impaired. But if he had real problems with a case, he would be in a hospital somewhere.

"One day we had a case where a man had been fencing outboard motors and we were waiting to start court but Brooks had checked himself into a hospital in Fort Walton. I happened to be in Judge Melvin's chambers when we got the word Brooks was in the hospital. So the judge called the doctor and in his usual calm manner asked him some questions. 'How is Brooks? We're concerned for his health.'"

The doctor responded, 'Oh, he's going to have some tests.'

'Well, how did he get to your facility? Was he taken by ambulance? Was it an emergency?'

'No, no, he just checked himself in.'

'Is it life threatening for Mr. Brooks to be over here in court?'

'No,' the doctor replied, 'I don't believe so.'

After gathering all the facts, Judge Melvin said, 'Doctor, please tell Mr. Brooks that if he's not here in my courtroom in an hour there will be a deputy sheriff to escort him in chains.' Brooks walked in an hour later.

"Butch went on to say, "One striking difference among judges today compared to Judge Melvin's time is that Woodrow could freely fraternize with all of the lawyers without fear of criticism. It would never occur to them that anybody was trying to get favoritism or that he would solicit such because they believed he was above that type of behavior.

"I can't imagine any lawyer having the nerve to try to curry favor with that judge because my guess would be it would have the wrong effect. I've always respected him and the office too much and so did everyone else. Ironically, that respect even found its way down to a defendant who had recently been released from prison.

"Before I started prosecuting, I went into this establishment where they served the best cheeseburgers in the world along with cold beer. Standing alongside the pool table was a man that had just served some time. I knew his family so I wasn't uncomfortable talking to him. Something came up in the conversation about prison and Judge Melvin. He immediately called him an old 'blankety-blank'! Then he shot the next pool ball and continued, 'But he was a fair old 'blankety-blank' 'cause I belonged in prison.'

"You have to imagine the tension that went from what he

first said to the absolute comic relief when he finished because there might have been some people there that thought the next thing they would hear would be a pool cue across somebody's head."

Butch was quick to add, "It was a known fact among the criminal element that the punishment given out by Judge Melvin was predictable. In Santa Rosa County, for armed robbery or threatening a person with a firearm, loaded or unloaded, you got to go to prison for life. Period.

"I confirmed this effect with an interview I had with an inmate who was being held in Escambia County for robbing convenient stores. It was suspected that he may have been responsible for such acts in Santa Rosa.

His response was immediate, 'Hell, no. I can do any number of armed robberies in Escambia County and go to jail, get sentenced to six or eight years and be out in three. That judge in Santa Rosa is crazy; if I did an armed robbery there and was caught, I'd be sent away forever.'

Butch commented, "That attitude kept our crime rate down over here because guys like him who were in the business of robbing Handi-Paks stayed out of Santa Rosa. Now, occasionally, we'd get one who was a rookie or just passin' through and he didn't know the rules and he'd stick something up."

Butch Lindsay's closing remarks express the respect and admiration he felt for Judge Melvin.

"He was the fairest and best I've ever seen. Now, he and I didn't always agree, but when we disagreed, he was right more times than I was because he knew more about what we were discussing. Judge Melvin could use knowledge better than any judge that I've ever seen before. The lawyers miss him and have for a long time because he could handle so many things efficiently. A lot of us got spoiled. I especially appreciated the fact that he played with one set of rules; the cases were tried and we moved on."

***

Reverend Joe Bamberg (deceased)

Much has been said about Woodrow's ability to communicate with others and develop relationships, but there was one relationship he initiated as a child and as he grew it matured into a private, personal bond between he and his Lord. Not one to flaunt his religion, the deep running faith he possessed silently filtered out into the details of his life.

Reverend Joe Bamberg, a retired pastor of the First Baptist Church in Milton, remembered Woodrow as an active participant in the congregation who served a four-year term as a deacon and taught classes from time to time.

Having known Woodrow since 1949, Reverend Bamberg saw a man of character who loved his family and never lost the common touch when associating with people.

A letter written to Woodrow in 1971 expressed his admiration.

> Dear Woody,
> It has been my privilege to sit in your court several times within the past year and I have been greatly impressed by the way you have conducted business.
> There is a dignity and gravity about the operation which is fitting to the serious nature of its affairs. Yet, at the same time, there is a proper deference shoed for the feelings of attorneys and clients in the ebb and flow of the action. The atmosphere is one that gives the impression that everyone is under control and yet the controls are not on so tight that everybody is tense.
> I believe your attempt to meet the needs and solve the problems of the youngsters that come before you is "just right". Your insistence upon discipline within the law and yet at the same time offering the youngster an opportunity to correct his error for the rehabilitation of his character is magnificent. There is the note of fatherly concern along with the respect for the rights of others as embodied in the law which gives a firmness but a kind

firmness.

Your treatment of the parents of these youngsters as you set forth the various circumstance surrounding the case in such a way that they may fully comprehend what is taking place—this treatment in kindness and patience and compassion is down-right impressive.

I am happy that you serve in this capacity and feel that your temperament, training and total philosophy of life make you admirably suited for this important position. Among many persons who feel this way, I remain

Your fellow-laborer,
Joe Bamberg

***

T. Sol Johnson
Attorney

T. Sol Johnson, son of A.L. Johnson, is a second generation attorney to practice before Judge Melvin.

"My first domestic case was memorable to me because I had only been practicing law for less than a month when a fellow walks into my office from Tampa looking to immediately take a lawyer with him across the street to the courthouse. I asked him what he was charged with and he told me contempt for nonpayment of child support.

"I explained that I needed time to prepare and he said that the hearing was in fifteen minutes and all he needed was an attorney to go with him. We went into Judge Melvin's chambers and he explained that he didn't have any money—hadn't sent any in six months. Judge Melvin let him finish and then in a tone of voice and a demeanor I came to recognize he became very focused and asked the fellow once more if there was anything else he needed to tell us. The man stumbled around and said, 'Judge, I just haven't had the money.'

Looking him right in the eye, Judge Melvin inquired, 'Have you sent them a loaf of bread?'

'No, Judge, I haven't.'

'Have you sent them a quart of milk?'

'No.'

'Have you sent them a dime?'

'No, sir.'

Woodrow turned around and dialed the intercom for the sheriff's office and simply said, 'Send me a deputy. I have a customer for you.'"

"As a novice attorney, I found out right away that this judge intended child support to be paid. He sent him straight to jail. He had the courage to make those decisions.

"One lawyer, T. Franklin West, found out that Judge Melvin was not easily intimidated. Woodrow had sentenced West's client to five years in the penitentiary after he was convicted. Franklin was known as someone who was persistent and kept bothering the judge about the sentence, He went beyond what most lawyers thought appropriate by contacting the judge's office. Finally, Judge Melvin relented and agreed to reconsider the sentence so the client had another sentencing and this time he gave him *ten* years. Later he went back to five but he made his point.

"One of the most profound and articulate statements I ever heard Judge Melvin make was to a defendant in a courtroom to a youth worker convicted of child molestation. Woodrow told him he viewed him as a cancer on society and he saw himself as the surgeon who was going to remove him for as long as he could and when he got out, if he ever got out, he would be so old that little children would not have to fear him when they walked passed him on the street.

"As an observer in the audience, I almost stood up and cheered.

"He was known as having a tremendous sense of fairness. We have smart judges who don't have a sense of fairness. They get choked up on the language of a particular paragraph and get the wrong result. Judge Melvin looked on the laws as a definition of right and wrong but not disassociated from right and wrong.

Sometimes it is not an easy thing to determine but he started out knowing what was right and wrong then he looked for an explanation in the statutes. Most defendants felt they would get a fair shake; he was never perceived as a hanging judge. He utilized his intellect and sense of fairness in such a way that it fostered the perception of a judicial system working right."

Part Five

Chapter Nineteen
Farewell, Your Honor

Woodrow Maxwell Melvin died November 25, 1994, following heart by-pass surgery at the age of 81.

A Santa Rosa oak tree fell on a warm and friendly afternoon recently; not tall in stature perhaps, but surely tall in kindness, good deeds and concern for justice.

Woodrow M. Melvin, Sr. was one of those rare men a community produces who stand head and shoulders above the rest, and by moving a branch illuminates the corner as well as the room; who balances justice with compassion; who never forgets he is first a human being and further down the list, a public official.

The oak tree fell—not from corruption within, or a rogue axe, nor a self-inflicted wound—but from a clock that spares no one. He will be missed.

Richard Barrett,
Editor, Press Gazette, Dec.1, 1994

The pews at Hickory Hammock Baptist Church were filled with family, friends, and peers wanting each in his or her own way to say good-bye and, if possible, capture one last moment with a dear friend.

After the funeral, a family acquaintance seeing the rows of judges, made this observation, "When I saw all those walking, black robes it reminded me of a graduation."

What a fitting metaphor; for surely Woodrow has graduated up to the highest, Supreme Court in the heavens to stand before the fairest and greatest Judge of all.

Made in the USA
Charleston, SC
05 March 2012